FIVE
INGREDIENT
VEGAN

For Carolyne and Mark

FIVE INGREDIENT VEGAN

100 SIMPLE, FAST, MODERN RECIPES

KATY BESKOW

Photography by Luke Albert

Hardie Grant

QUADRILLE

Introduction

It's often thought that vegan cooking is complicated, with some recipes requiring multiple ingredients, advanced cooking techniques and hours spent in the kitchen. In reality, who has the time (or inclination) for that? I know that after a hard day of work, the last thing anyone wants to do is follow a never-ending list of ingredients and chef's-style recipe method, which is why I've put together this book of simplified meals that are full of flavour and substance, despite their minimal ingredients lists.

Five Ingredient Vegan shows you how to cook a range of tasty meals using just five ingredients, all of which can be purchased from a supermarket; in fact it's likely that you'll already have most of the ingredients in your store cupboard! To get the best out of these recipes, I've assumed that you have three basic kitchen ingredients: oil, sea salt and black pepper.

At a time when vegan cooking may seem overcomplicated and unachievable, let these recipes help you fall in love with making delicious meals. Whether you are vegan or just want to try a few vegan recipes, this book will show you how to make the most of your time in the kitchen, without having to shop for obscure, unpronounceable

ingredients. I've included plenty of tips along the way, to make the process easy and fuss free, and also tested which recipes can be frozen without compromising their flavour or texture.

The recipes are organized into five chapters: Soups, Lunches, Suppers, Sweets and Basics; you'll find recipes for all of the family to enjoy! Feeling confident in the kitchen comes with building up your own repertoire of meals that you enjoy cooking. It is so rewarding to be able to create and present hearty, fresh and nourishing dishes (with a few treats too!).

I'm a firm believer that a few simple, good-quality ingredients can make the most satisfying of home-cooked meals. Buy the best that you can afford, particularly fresh ingredients such as vegetables, fruit and bread, and aim to buy ingredients in season for maximum flavour.

Strip it back, keep it simple and think about versatile ways to use your fresh and store-cupboard ingredients to create something memorable every day of the week.

Five ways to keep it simple in the kitchen

Whether you're a confident cook, or a not-so-confident home cook, keeping it simple in the kitchen will allow you to create something delicious, with minimal effort and maximum enjoyment. Follow these five tips and let simple cooking change the way you view meal preparation.

1 USE RECIPES WITH JUST A FEW INGREDIENTS

Choose recipes with up to five ingredients, to keep cooking simple and fuss free. You can then get creative by adding extra ingredients to the basic recipe, depending on what you have available and what flavours you want to add in. Having a collection of simple base recipes will build your confidence to develop dishes to suit your personal tastes. For many of the recipes, I've made suggestions about additional ingredients to offer variety, but feel free to explore your own ideas!

2 BUY VERSATILE INGREDIENTS

When buying an ingredient or some fresh produce, think about how you can use it all; not only will you cut down on food waste and keep money in your pocket, but you'll have an overall appreciation of food production efforts. For example, baby spinach leaves are wonderful raw in a salad, they make a colourful addition to a dhal and boost the nutritional values of soup. If you will only use a small quantity of an ingredient, consider buying it frozen so that you can save the rest for another time without it going to waste – sweetcorn or berries are perfect to stash in your freezer.

3 BATCH COOK

Whether you have some spare time, or have simply made too large a quantity of food for your needs, it's worth keeping leftovers or extra portions in the fridge or freezer to save you cooking again after a busy day. I've added a note to each recipe to state if it is suitable for freezing, or storage suggestions for longevity. I keep a stock of clean jars and plastic containers available for batch cooking, but don't forget to label the container to remind you what it is (it can be hard to tell when it's frozen!). As standard, I always have a supply of versatile tomato sauce (page 207), lime curd (page 155) and mushroom gravy (page 211) available to cover all meal and snack bases.

4 KEEP KEY EQUIPMENT TO HAND

Before you start cooking, read through the recipe and decide what equipment you need to use, then have it accessible to make the process as simple and streamlined as possible. This may mean laying out a pan, wooden spoon, hand whisk and knife along with the ingredients prior to beginning a recipe. The stress of finding that box grater at the back of the cupboard while stirring a sauce is one that is easily avoided with just a couple of minutes of preparation.

5 HAVE FUN

Whether you're cooking alone, with a partner or with children, enjoy your time and experiences in the kitchen. Take yourself on a journey with new ingredients, absorb the aromas and sounds and enjoy learning how a dish is brought together. Failing that, put on some music, pour yourself a glass of wine or a cup of tea and get cooking!

Store-cupboard essentials

In this book, I have assumed that you have three basic ingredients – oil, sea salt and black pepper – so these ingredients are not included in the ingredient count for each recipe, allowing the five main ingredients to be the stars of the show! Keep a stock of a few essential store-cupboard ingredients, alongside fresh produce, for delicious and balanced meals.

OILS

Sunflower is my choice of oil for cooking, as it is flavourless and has a high smoke point. This makes it versatile to use for roasting, sautéing and frying – it's also great value for money. Good-quality extra virgin olive oil is perfect for dressing salads, drizzling over pasta and as a dip for bread. Store both of these oils in a cool, dark cupboard to preserve their quality and flavour.

SEA SALT AND BLACK PEPPER

Opt for good-quality sea salt flakes; when used sparingly they enhance the finished flavour of any dish – just lightly crush between your fingers when sprinkling. Occasionally, I've suggested using smoked sea salt, which is widely available now; it can add another level of flavour to your dishes but can easily be substituted with normal sea salt. Freshly ground black pepper is a great way to finish a dish to add a pop of flavour and that familiar heat.

CANS OF BEANS AND PULSES

Keep a selection of canned chickpeas (garbanzo beans), lentils, jackfruit and red kidney beans to hand so that you can whip up a meal with very little preparation, soaking or boiling times. These ingredients have a long shelf life, meaning they're a handy essential to have available. Simply pour away the canned water and rinse thoroughly in cold water to avoid any 'canned' taste. Edamame and broad beans can be used in cooking from frozen; their texture and flavour is unaffected by the freezing process and it means less waste too – use only what you need before returning the rest to the freezer.

DRIED PULSES, GRAINS, RICE AND FLOUR

Complement speedy canned pulses with some dried pulses and grains, including yellow split peas, red split lentils and bulgar wheat. Rice, oats and flour are also helpful ingredients to have available too. Store these in glass jars in a cool, dark place for longevity and easy accessibility when you need them.

PASTA

Most dried pasta available in supermarkets is actually egg free, so there's no need to source specialist pasta, but do always check the ingredients before buying. Avoid fresh pasta, as this is likely to contain eggs. If you have the space available, keep a stock of small soup pasta, bite-sized penne or fusilli and ribbon pasta such as tagliatelle or pappardelle; you'll have every pasta-based meal covered!

CHOPPED TOMATOES AND PASSATA

Have a stock of good-quality chopped tomatoes ready to use as a base for curries, chilli and casseroles. Passata is chopped tomatoes that have been sieved until smooth, ideal for silky sauces and soups. Pick up some passata with added herbs and garlic to combine flavours in one easy step. Tomato purée (paste) adds a concentrated burst of flavour to tomato-based dishes, but substitute with tomato ketchup, which is concentrated and seasoned, if you don't have purée available.

HERB AND SPICE BLENDS

Alongside your favourite staple dried herbs and spices, choose a few pre-blended mixes that will save you shelf space instead of having many individual ingredients. These may include dried mixed herbs, Cajun seasoning, ras el hanout and rose harissa paste, which will pack a flavour punch in just one sprinkling or spoonful. As a general rule, woody herbs such as sage, rosemary and thyme taste great when dried, but buy fresh leafy herbs such as flat-leaf parsley, basil and coriander (cilantro) to get the best flavour out of them.

FRUITS AND VEGETABLES

Choose quality fresh produce, and where possible pick fruits and vegetables that are in season for the best flavour, texture and price. Eating seasonally and choosing different fruits and vegetables will ensure you won't get bored of cooking the same recipes every week! Keep fruits and vegetables chilled or cool for longevity and freshness, bringing them to room temperature before using to bring out their best flavours and juices. Always keep a supply of onions, garlic and potatoes nearby, as these work well as a foundation for many meals, then choose other vegetables and fruits based on seasonality and what looks vibrant. Don't overlook fresh leafy herbs: basil, flat-leaf parsley and coriander (cilantro) can lift the flavours in one easy step. Many vegetables cook well from frozen including peas, spinach, leeks and butternut squash.

NON-DAIRY ALTERNATIVES

You'll find a range of non-dairy milks available in supermarkets including soya, almond, rice and oat, so it's good to try a few and choose your favourite. I find unsweetened soya milk to be the most versatile for drinks and cooking, while vanilla-flavoured soya milk is great to use as a sweet baking ingredient. Soya or coconut yogurts are versatile, working well as a cool dressing over curry, chilli and tagine, and deliciously with sweet breakfasts and desserts. Vegan cheeses are available in large supermarkets, from mild cream cheese to hard vegan Parmesan.

The minimal kitchen

To create nourishing home-cooked food, you don't need a kitchen full to the brim with specialist equipment and devices. Just a few versatile tools will do the job. It's also worth considering where you will store any equipment, to avoid unnecessary clutter on your worktops. A basic kitchen should have a fridge, oven and hob, and a small selection of tools and serving dishes.

FREEZER

This kitchen essential allows you to store freshly frozen products for speedy or occasional use. You can also freeze suitable leftovers in individual portions (using freezer and microwave/oven-safe containers) for convenient meals with no waste. Make batches of essential base recipes, such as versatile tomato sauce (page 207) for quick and easy use when you need them most.

CUPBOARD SPACE

We're not all blessed with a pantry to store endless products, but do dedicate at least one cupboard to cans, dried spices and herbs, grains and rice. I like to store flour, sugar, rice, grains and nuts in glass jars for freshness and ease of use, without having to reseal bags (and to reduce the risk of spillage!). Keep the cupboard as organized as possible, with clear labelling to make selecting your ingredients a breeze.

KNIVES

Choose weighty, good-quality knives that fit ergonomically in your hand, for easy chopping, slicing and dicing. A home kitchen does not need a huge selection of knives; one small, medium and large knife, as well as a bread knife, will serve all your needs. Buy the best you can afford, and look after them for an investment that extends well into the future. Use a wooden chopping board to avoid damage to your knives and make ingredient preparation easy.

BLENDER

High-powered jug blenders are ideal for whipping up the silkiest soups, sauces and spice mixes (blenders are for so much more than smoothies!), but they can take up vital kitchen space. A simple hand blender is a space saver, but will require a little more time and effort to achieve a smooth result.

PANS

As with knives, a minimal home kitchen does not require multiple pans. As a rule, a couple of medium and large pans, alongside a wok, frying and griddle pan, will help you to cook versatile meals. Wash in soap and water, avoiding the use of scratchy scouring pads, which can damage non-stick linings.

WOODEN SPOON

Often overlooked, the humble wooden spoon is a kitchen hero. Perfect to use when stirring hot dishes, the heat is not transferred through the wood, to keep your hand safe from burns. They also protect your pans from scratches that can happen if using metal or plastic spoons, and are good for scraping sauces from blender jugs, as well as for mixing when baking.

MEASURING SPOONS AND SCALES

A set of measuring spoons ensures accuracy when using tablespoon and teaspoon measurements. They are cheap to purchase and straightforward to use and store. Opt for digital, flat weighing scales for ease of use and small-space storage.

MICROWAVE OVEN

Microwaves are great for reheating leftover food safely, warming non-dairy milk for your cocoa and making cakes in minutes, as in the Victoria sponge mug cake (page 159). You can also heat lemons and limes for a few seconds to release more juice and flavour from the fruits, and even sterilize a damp kitchen cloth!

SOUPS

Keep a selection of simple soup recipes to hand for when you need something warming and wholesome. Many of these soups are suitable for freezing, so create a batch and freeze in portion-sized containers, for those times when only a comforting bowl of goodness will satisfy.

Pantry minestrone

SERVES 4

Suitable for freezing

1 tbsp olive oil

———

1 **leek**, very thinly sliced

———

2 **carrots**, peeled and halved lengthways, then chopped

———

300ml (10fl oz) **versatile tomato sauce** (see page 207); store-bought is also fine

———

4 tbsp dried **margheritine soup pasta**, or any other small pasta (ensure egg free)

———

small handful of frozen or fresh **peas**

———

generous pinch of sea salt and black pepper

———

Who would have thought that comforting minestrone could be made with just five ingredients? I love simmering this soup at that point in the week when I'm running out of fresh supplies, or at the end of the month when the bank balance is running low!

Heat the oil in a large pan, add the leek and carrots and cook over a medium heat for at least 5 minutes until the carrots begin to soften.

Pour in the tomato sauce and 1 litre (1¾ pints) just-boiled water, then simmer for 10 minutes.

Add the pasta and cook for a further 10 minutes.

Stir through the peas and cook for 2 minutes. Remove from the heat and season generously to taste with sea salt and black pepper.

TIPS
If you don't have any versatile tomato sauce (page 207) available, add a crushed garlic clove along with the leek, then 1 teaspoon of dried basil or oregano and 400g (14oz) canned chopped tomatoes.

Spiced parsnip bisque

SERVES 4

Suitable for freezing

500g (1lb 2oz) **parsnips**, peeled and roughly chopped

1 **onion**, quartered

2 tbsp sunflower oil

1 tsp **garam masala**

400ml (14fl oz) canned **coconut milk**

500ml (18fl oz) hot **vegetable stock** (page 212)

generous pinch of sea salt and black pepper

The whole family will love this gently spiced soup, which is perfectly warming for autumn and winter months. Coconut milk gives a silky-smooth texture to the bisque, which tastes utterly decadent when combined with sweet roasted parsnips and mild spices.

Preheat the oven to 200°C/400°F/gas mark 6.

Place the parsnips and onion in a roasting tin and drizzle with the oil. Roast in the oven for 30 minutes until golden and softened.

Remove the roasted parsnips and onion from the oven, and spoon into a high-powered jug blender (or into a large pan if you are using a hand blender). Add the garam masala, then pour in the coconut milk and hot vegetable stock. Blitz until completely smooth. Season to taste with sea salt and black pepper.

Ladle into warmed bowls and serve hot, sprinkled with a little extra garam masala and black pepper, if you like.

TIPS

Garam masala is a spice blend that often contains cumin, cinnamon, curry leaves, coriander seed, cardamom and cloves. Add to homemade curries and samosas for instant flavour. You'll find it in the spice aisle at the supermarket.

Leek and potato soup

SERVES 4

Suitable for freezing

1 tbsp sunflower oil

———————

2 medium **leeks**, thinly sliced

———————

3 medium **baking potatoes**, peeled and evenly diced

———————

800ml (28fl oz) hot **vegetable stock** (page 212)

———————

400ml (14fl oz) **unsweetened soya milk**

———————

generous pinch of sea salt and black pepper

———————

I like to think of this soup as a hug in a bowl. The familiar, homely flavours and creamy texture are comforting and warming – and what's more, it freezes perfectly, so you'll have homemade soup whenever you need it.

Heat the oil in a large pan, add the leeks and cook over a medium heat for at least 5 minutes until softened.

Add the diced potatoes and pour in the vegetable stock. Simmer for 20 minutes, with the pan lid placed loosely over, until the potatoes have softened.

Remove from the heat, then pour in the soya milk. Ladle into a high-powered jug blender (or use a hand blender) and blitz until completely smooth.

Generously season to taste with sea salt and black pepper.

TIPS

A high-powered jug blender will blitz the ingredients into a creamy, silky soup in no time. If you are using a hand blender, it may take a little longer to reach the desired consistency.

Charred courgette soup

SERVES 4

Suitable for freezing

1 tbsp sunflower oil

———

2 medium **courgettes (zucchini)**, sliced lengthways

———

1 **onion**, roughly chopped

———

2 medium **baking potatoes**, peeled and evenly diced

———

1 litre (1¾ pints) hot **vegetable stock** (page 212)

———

handful of **flat-leaf parsley**, finely chopped

———

generous pinch of smoked sea salt and black pepper

———

If you've ever been left disappointed by a courgette soup, give this fail-safe recipe a go. Slightly charring the courgettes brings a subtle, smoky flavour to the soup, while flat-leaf parsley balances the taste with summery freshness. Adding potato gives a thick and creamy texture when blended.

Heat the oil in a large griddle pan, add the courgettes in batches and cook over a high heat until softened and charred on both sides.

Put the courgettes in a dish to one side, then add the onion to the pan and cook over a high heat for 5–6 minutes until gently browned. Stir occasionally to avoid sticking.

Add the courgettes, onion, potatoes and vegetable stock to a large pan and simmer over a medium heat for 25 minutes until the potatoes have softened.

Remove from the heat, ladle into a high-powered jug blender (or use a hand blender) and blitz on high until completely smooth.

Stir through the flat-leaf parsley and season to taste with smoked sea salt and black pepper.

TIPS
This recipe can be easily doubled if you're faced with a seasonal glut of courgettes.

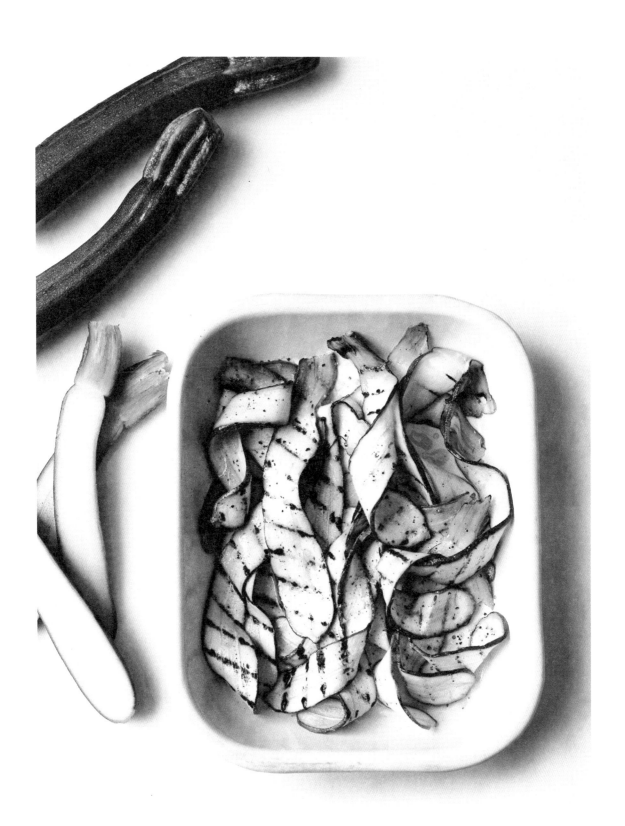

Cauliflower cheese soup

SERVES 4

Suitable for freezing

1 medium **cauliflower**, broken into florets, outer leaves removed

———

1 tbsp sunflower oil

———

3 tbsp vegan **cream cheese**

———

500ml (18fl oz) hot **vegetable stock** (page 212)

———

300ml (10fl oz) **unsweetened soya milk**

———

handful of **chives**, finely chopped

———

generous pinch of sea salt and black pepper

———

Combine two comfort classics – baked cauliflower cheese and a bowl of steamy soup! You'd never believe that this rich and creamy soup could be vegan, or be so easy to prepare. This is a firm family favourite, from my table to yours.

Preheat the oven to 180°C/350°F/gas mark 4.

Arrange the cauliflower florets on a baking tray and drizzle with the sunflower oil. Roast in the oven for 20–25 minutes until golden and softened.

Remove the roasted cauliflower from the oven and carefully spoon into a high-powered jug blender. Add the vegan cream cheese, vegetable stock and soya milk, then blitz on high until silky smooth. (If you're using a hand blender, add the above ingredients to a large bowl, then blitz until completely smooth.)

Stir through the chives and season with sea salt and black pepper to taste. Serve in warmed bowls, sprinkled with a few extra chopped chives and black pepper, and drizzled with a little extra virgin olive oil, if you like.

TIPS

You'll find vegan cream cheese in most supermarkets, often in the chilled 'free from' section. There are many varieties and brands to choose from; a simple mild cream cheese works best for this recipe.

Country lentil pottage

SERVES 4
GENEROUSLY

Suitable for freezing

300g (10oz) dried **red split lentils**, rinsed in cold water

2 **baking potatoes**, peeled and evenly diced

4 **carrots**, peeled and grated

1 **onion**, finely chopped

2 litres (3½ pints) hot **vegetable stock** (page 212)

generous pinch of sea salt and black pepper

This isn't the type of soup that should be blended to creamy smoothness – it's rustic, chunky and oh-so homely. Celebrate this country pottage by serving with warm crusty bread, fresh from the oven, such as my 3-ingredient beer bread (page 195) pictured, spread with vegan butter.

Put the lentils, potatoes, carrots, onion and vegetable stock into a large pan. Bring to the boil, then simmer for 40–45 minutes, stirring occasionally to avoid sticking.

When the lentils have broken down, remove from the heat and season to taste with sea salt and black pepper.

TIPS

This one-step soup will become a family favourite, as it is simple to make and freezes well for up to 3 months – perfect for those times when you just need a quick and easy bowl of something satisfying.

Tomato and chilli soup

SERVES 4

Suitable for freezing

1 tbsp sunflower oil

———

1 **onion**, diced

———

½ tsp dried **chilli flakes**

———

400g (14oz) good-quality
canned **chopped tomatoes**

———

500ml (18fl oz) hot
vegetable stock (page 212)

———

pinch of **caster
(superfine) sugar**

———

generous pinch of sea salt
and black pepper

———

**In need of something warming? This creamy tomato
soup has a hint of fiery chilli to satisfy taste buds and
tummies on colder days. Fill up a flask for perfectly
portable comfort food! Serve sprinkled with my black
pepper croutons (page 203) for added crunch.**

Heat the oil in a large pan, add the onion and chilli flakes
and cook over a medium heat for 3–4 minutes until the
onion has softened but not browned.

Pour in the chopped tomatoes, vegetable stock and sugar,
then simmer for 15 minutes.

Pour into a high-powered jug blender (or use a hand
blender) and blitz until completely smooth and creamy.
Season to taste with sea salt and black pepper.

TIPS
Add more or fewer chilli flakes, to suit your taste.

Pasta e fagioli

SERVES 4

Suitable for freezing

1 tbsp sunflower oil

―――――

1 **onion**, finely chopped

―――――

500g (1lb 2oz) **passata**
with herbs

―――――

300g (10oz) canned **cannellini
beans**, drained and rinsed

―――――

4 tbsp **margheritine soup
pasta**, or any other small
pasta (ensure egg free)

―――――

800ml (28fl oz) hot
vegetable stock (page 212)

―――――

generous pinch of sea salt
and black pepper

―――――

**This simple Italian peasant dish means 'pasta and beans'
and has more of a soupy texture than that of a stew.
It uses inexpensive, store-cupboard ingredients and
is ready in 20 minutes, making this a go-to staple.**

Heat the oil in a large pan, add the onion and cook over
a medium heat for 5 minutes until softened.

Pour in the passata, cannellini beans, pasta and hot
vegetable stock, then simmer for 15 minutes until the
pasta has softened.

Remove from the heat and season to taste with sea salt
and black pepper.

TIPS

If you don't have passata with herbs available, simply
add 1 teaspoon of dried oregano with the onion and
use plain passata.

Chestnut mushroom soup

SERVES 4

Suitable for freezing

1 tbsp sunflower oil

500g (1lb 2oz) **chestnut (cremini) mushrooms**, brushed clean and sliced

2 **garlic** cloves, crushed

500ml (18fl oz) hot **vegetable stock** (page 212)

200ml (7fl oz) **unsweetened soya milk**

handful of **flat-leaf parsley**, roughly chopped

pinch of sea salt and black pepper

This is simple comfort food that will nourish and warm body and soul. Chestnut mushrooms have a rich, slightly nutty flavour that is perfect for this soup. I love to swirl a spoonful of unsweetened soya yogurt through just before serving – the creamy, cool yogurt is a beautiful contrast to the hot, earthy soup.

Heat the oil in a large pan, add the mushrooms and cook over a medium–high heat for 10 minutes until they have softened and become fragrant. Stir in the garlic and cook for a further minute. Spoon out a tablespoon of the cooked mushrooms, and set aside to use as a garnish later.

Pour in the vegetable stock and simmer for 10 minutes. Remove from the heat and pour in the soya milk. Ladle into a high-powered jug blender (or use a hand blender) and blitz until completely smooth.

Stir through the flat-leaf parsley and season to taste with sea salt and plenty of black pepper. Ladle into bowls and garnish with the reserved garlic mushrooms.

Spicy noodle soup

SERVES 2

400ml (14fl oz) canned full-fat **coconut milk**

---

1 heaped tbsp **red Thai curry paste** (ensure fish free)

300g (10oz) ready-to-wok soft **noodles** (ensure egg free)

---

2 **spring onions (scallions)**, finely shredded

---

small handful of **coriander (cilantro)**, roughly torn

Dig into this spiced, fragrant soup as a substantial lunch or even a warming but light evening dinner. Red Thai curry paste packs a flavour punch with a kick of chilli – do read the ingredients thoroughly, as some contain fish sauce. Serve with chopsticks (or a fork) to eat the noodles, as well as a spoon to sip the spicy broth!

In a large pan, heat the coconut milk and red Thai curry paste for 10 minutes until combined and simmering. Pour in 250ml (9fl oz) just-boiled water and continue to simmer.

Put the noodles into the pan, then cook for a further 5 minutes until softened and separated.

Ladle into bowls and garnish with the spring onions and coriander. Serve immediately.

Carrot and coriander velouté

SERVES 4

Suitable for freezing

1 tbsp sunflower oil
_____

1 **onion**, roughly chopped
_____

6 large **carrots**, peeled
and roughly chopped
_____

400ml (14fl oz) canned full-fat
coconut milk
_____

700ml (1¼ pints) hot
vegetable stock (page 212)
_____

generous handful of **coriander
(cilantro)**, finely chopped
_____

generous pinch of sea salt
and black pepper
_____

**Make this soup when you're looking to impress. Serve at
the start of an elegant meal as a small bowl of creamy
and rich velouté. The coconut milk is essential for a silky-
smooth texture that is luxurious and decadent. Delicious
served with seedy crackers or slices of buttered bread.**

Add the oil, onion and carrots to a large pan and cook
over a medium–high heat for 5 minutes until the carrot
begins to soften.

Pour in the coconut milk and vegetable stock, then simmer
for 20 minutes.

Remove from the heat, ladle into a high-powered jug
blender (or use a hand blender) and blitz until completely
smooth. Double blend if necessary to ensure the velouté
is completely blended and silky.

Stir through the chopped coriander and season to taste
with sea salt and black pepper. Serve in warmed bowls.

Lemony super greens soup

SERVES 4

Suitable for freezing

1 medium head of **broccoli**, broken into florets

—————

2 handfuls of **spinach**

—————

4 tbsp frozen or fresh **peas**

—————

generous handful of **mint** leaves

—————

juice of 2 unwaxed **lemons**

—————

generous pinch of sea salt and black pepper

—————

After a weekend of treats and late nights, I love to whip up this soup for some Monday nourishment. Packed with vitamins, minerals and protein, this soup is deliciously brightened with lemon juice.

Bring 800ml (28fl oz) water to the boil in a large pan. Add the broccoli florets, spinach and peas and simmer for 15 minutes until the broccoli has softened. Add the mint leaves and remove from the heat.

Ladle the vegetables and the cooking water into a high-powered jug blender (or use a hand blender) and blitz until completely smooth.

Stir through the lemon juice and season to taste with sea salt and black pepper.

TIPS
Serve this soup hot, or chilled as a refreshing gazpacho.

Harissa chickpea soup

SERVES 2

Suitable for freezing

1 tbsp sunflower oil

_____

1 large **onion**, diced

_____

2 tsp **rose harissa paste**

_____

400g (14oz) good-quality canned **chopped tomatoes**

_____

400g (14oz) canned **chickpeas (garbanzo beans)**, drained and rinsed

_____

generous handful of **flat-leaf parsley**, torn

_____

generous pinch of sea salt

_____

This fragrant, warming soup is perfect for serving with easy flatbreads (page 194). It also freezes very well, making it a convenient light bite, whenever you need it.

Heat the oil in a large pan, add the onion and cook for 2–3 minutes over a medium heat until softened but not browned. Spoon in the harissa paste and cook for a further minute.

Pour in the chopped tomatoes and chickpeas, along with 200ml (7fl oz) just-boiled water. Simmer over a medium heat for 15–20 minutes.

Remove from the heat and stir in the flat-leaf parsley. Season with sea salt to taste.

TIPS

No longer exclusive to Middle Eastern shops, rose harissa is now available in most supermarkets. It is a spice blend containing chillies, herbs and dried rose petals, and gives depth, fragrance and heat to Moroccan-inspired dishes including the Harissa-yogurt whole roasted cauliflower with pomegranate and pistachios (page 97).

Salsa gazpacho

SERVES 2

1 small **red onion**, finely diced

200g (7oz) **cherry tomatoes**, finely chopped

handful of **coriander (cilantro)**, finely chopped

generous pinch of sea salt and balck pepper

500g (1lb 2oz) **passata**

juice of 1 unwaxed **lime**

Nothing beats a cool, refreshing gazpacho on a summer's day. This version combines the fresh and vibrant flavours of salsa, with coriander and lime bringing fragrance and zing. Pre-soaking the onion removes the acidity, for all the flavour without the sharpness.

Place the diced red onion in a small bowl and cover with just-boiled water. Allow to stand for 15 minutes, then drain away the water.

Add the onion to a large bowl and mix with the tomatoes and coriander. Season with a pinch of sea salt and black pepper. Pour in the passata and lime juice and mix.

Refrigerate for at least 2 hours before serving in chilled bowls or glasses.

TIPS This gazpacho will keep in the fridge for up to 3 days.

Roasted onion soup

SERVES 4

Suitable for freezing

6 **onions**, thickly sliced

―――――――

2 tbsp sunflower oil

―――――――

1 litre (1¾ pints)
vegetable stock (page 212)

―――――――

1 whole sprig of **thyme**

―――――――

1 tsp **Dijon mustard**

―――――――

small handful of **flat-leaf
parsley**, finely chopped

―――――――

generous pinch of sea salt
and black pepper

―――――――

**This effortless soup is comforting and delicious, without
having to pan-caramelize the onions. Roasting the onions
until golden brown gives the soup its traditional colour,
while the addition of mustard is a nod to its French
origins. Serve with vegan cheese melted on toast.**

Preheat the oven to 180°C/350°F/gas mark 4.

Arrange the sliced onion in a roasting tin and drizzle
over the oil, coating all of the onion. Roast in the oven
for 35-40 minutes until caramelized and browned without
being burned.

Bring the vegetable stock to a simmer in a large pan.
Spoon in the roasted onions, add the thyme sprig and stir
through the mustard. Simmer for 10 minutes.

Carefully remove the thyme sprig and take the pan off the
heat. Stir through the chopped parsley and season to taste
with sea salt and black pepper.

LUNCHES

Life is too short for boring lunches, so whip yourself up one of these no-fuss midday meals. Whether you have time for a hot lunch, or need to take out a packed lunch, there's something for everyone in this chapter.

Cumin-roasted cauliflower and mango salad

SERVES 2 GENEROUSLY

1 **cauliflower**, broken
into florets

———

1 tbsp sunflower oil

———

½ tsp ground **cumin**

———

1 **mango**, peeled, stoned
and sliced into ribbons
using a vegetable peeler

———

2 generous handfuls of
watercress

———

small handful of **coriander
(cilantro)**, roughly torn

———

pinch of sea salt
and black pepper

———

Lightly spiced and roasted cauliflower, sweet mango ribbons, coriander and always-pretty watercress are combined in this refreshing lunch that is delicious either warm or cold, in any season.

Preheat the oven to 220°C/425°F/gas mark 7 and arrange the cauliflower florets evenly on a baking tray.

In a small bowl, mix together the oil and ground cumin. Use a pastry brush to coat the cauliflower with the cumin oil. Bake in the oven for 15–20 minutes until golden and crisp at the edges.

In the meantime, toss the mango ribbons, watercress and coriander together on a serving plate.

Carefully remove the roasted cauliflower florets from the oven and toss into the salad. Season with sea salt and black pepper and drizzle over any hot oil from the tray.

TIPS

For added protein and extra crunch, scatter a few toasted flaked almonds over the salad.

Coronation chickpeas

SERVES 2 GENEROUSLY

400g (14oz) canned
chickpeas (garbanzo beans),
drained and rinsed

———————

2 tbsp vegan **mayonnaise**

———————

2 tsp **mango chutney**

———————

1 tsp mild **curry powder**

———————

small handful of **coriander
(cilantro)**, roughly torn

———————

pinch of sea salt
and black pepper

———————

**Delicately spiced, creamy and fruity, these chickpeas
are a modern twist on the classic. Use to fill a baguette,
or to load into a baked potato. How golden the overall
colour will be depends on the quantity of turmeric in the
curry powder, as all brands vary – add a pinch of ground
turmeric for added vibrancy of colour, if desired.**

Tip the chickpeas into a large bowl and roughly mash
some of them with the back of a fork.

Spoon in the vegan mayonnaise, mango chutney and
curry powder and stir to combine until the mashed
chickpeas are coated.

Stir through the coriander, season to taste with sea salt
and black pepper and then refrigerate for up to an hour
to allow the flavours to infuse.

TIPS

For added texture and crunch, stir through 1 tablespoon
of flaked almonds

No-fish cakes

MAKES ABOUT 10

4 **baking potatoes**, peeled
and roughly chopped

———

400g (14oz) canned **jackfruit**,
drained and rinsed

———

4 tbsp vegan **mayonnaise**

———

2 **spring onions (scallions)**,
very finely chopped

———

generous handful of **flat-leaf
parsley**, very finely chopped

———

generous pinch of sea salt
and black pepper

———

4 tbsp sunflower oil

———

**All the flavour and texture of fish cakes – but completely
vegan! These no-fish cakes are golden and crisp on
the outside, while being fluffy and fragrant inside. The
secret? Canned jackfruit. Jackfruit is a fruit grown in
South Asia; it has a naturally meaty texture and is able
to absorb flavours well. It is now widely available in large
supermarkets, Asian supermarkets and health-food
shops, sold canned or vacuum-packed. I love serving
these with wedges of lemon for squeezing, and a little
unsweetened soya yogurt, sprinkled with fresh dill.**

Bring a pan of water to the boil and add the potatoes.
Boil for 20–25 minutes until softened. Drain, then return to
the pan and mash until smooth. Allow the mashed potato
to cool to a temperature that is comfortable to handle.

Separate the chunks of jackfruit into strands, discarding
any tough parts. Add the strands to the pan along with the
mayonnaise, spring onions and parsley. Season with salt
and pepper, then stir to combine all of the ingredients.

Once combined, take heaped tablespoon-sized amounts
of the mixture and shape into patties about 5–6cm (2–2½in)
in diameter. Place on a plate, then refrigerate for 1 hour
(this will help to firm them up for easier cooking).

Heat the sunflower oil in a frying pan until hot. Carefully
add up to four of the patties to the pan and cook over a
medium–high heat for 5 minutes until golden, then use
tongs to turn them over and cook for a further 5 minutes.
Remove from the pan and keep warm while you cook the
remaining no-fish cakes. Serve hot.

TIPS
Cook the no-fish cakes in two batches to avoid overfilling
the pan, making turning easier and ensuring even cooking.

Aubergine tempura

SERVES 2 GENEROUSLY

200ml (7fl oz) sunflower oil, for deep-frying

—————

100g (3½oz) **plain (all-purpose) flour**

—————

50g (2oz) **cornflour (cornstarch)**

—————

½ tsp **baking powder**

—————

200ml (7fl oz) ice-cold **sparkling water**

—————

2 medium **aubergines (eggplants)**, thinly sliced, large slices halved

—————

Piping hot, crisp and ready to dip, aubergine tempura makes an ideal lunch. It's often believed that tempura is tricky to make, but it couldn't be simpler. The key to tempura perfection is to use ice-cold sparkling water in the batter and, by contrast, to make sure the oil for deep-frying is extremely hot!

Pour the oil into a large pan and place over a medium heat to heat up while you prepare the batter.

In a wide bowl, combine the flour, cornflour and baking powder. Stir in the sparkling water and use a balloon whisk to gently beat until smooth.

Check if the oil is hot enough by dropping in a blob of batter – if it sizzles immediately, the oil is ready.

Dip the aubergine slices into the batter and shake off any excess. Using a slotted spoon, add a few slices of aubergine to the very hot oil. Do not add too many slices at a time, as they will mass together. Deep-fry for 2–3 minutes until the batter has become crisp and puffed.

Carefully remove from the hot oil and drain on paper towels while you cook the remaining aubergine slices. Serve hot with your choice of dipping sauce.

TIPS
Soy sauce makes a deliciously simple dip, or serve with satay sauce (page 209).

Spinach pancakes with cream cheese and chives

SERVES 2 GENEROUSLY
(MAKES ABOUT 6)

100g (3½oz) **plain
(all-purpose) flour**

————

180ml (6fl oz) **unsweetened
soya milk**, chilled

————

generous handful
of **spinach**

————

generous pinch of sea salt
and black pepper

————

6 tbsp sunflower oil

————

3 heaped tbsp vegan
cream cheese

————

small handful of **chives**,
very finely chopped

————

Who doesn't love a pancake? Blending spinach into the batter gives the pancakes a gorgeous green hue, which little diners just love too. I often serve them with a lemon wedge for squeezing over.

Add the flour, soya milk, spinach leaves and sea salt to a high-powered jug blender or food processor and blitz until you have a smooth green batter.

Heat 1 tablespoon of the oil in a frying pan over a medium–high heat. Test if the oil is hot by adding a drop of the pancake batter to the pan; if it sizzles and becomes golden within 30 seconds, the oil is at the optimum temperature. Add about a ladleful of batter to the pan to make one pancake, swirling the batter around the pan to coat the base evenly.

When the pancake becomes slightly crisp after 2–3 minutes, carefully flip it onto the other side and cook for a further 2–3 minutes. Drain on paper towels and keep warm while you cook the remaining pancakes, adding a tablespoon of oil to the pan each time.

In a small bowl, stir together the vegan cream cheese and the chives. Spread or spoon the cream cheese onto the pancakes and serve, sprinkled with a few extra chopped chives, if you like, and a pinch of black pepper.

TIPS
Vegan cream cheese is available from most supermarkets – there are so many brands and varieties to choose from, so try them all and decide which is your favourite!

Sicilian pizza muffins

1 tbsp sunflower oil

———

1 small **aubergine (eggplant)**, thinly sliced

———

1 **red onion**, thinly sliced into rings

———

4 plain **English muffins**, halved

———

4 tbsp **tomato purée (paste)** with herbs

———

small handful of **basil** leaves

———

generous pinch of sea salt and black pepper

———

Ever wanted to create that bready, light pizza base, just the way the Sicilians do? This is the perfect cheat! English muffins make a quick and simple Sicilian-style base for you to add your favourite toppings to. I love the simplicity of pan-softened aubergines and red onion, but load up with sultanas, pine nuts, rocket (arugula) and lemon juice for an extra-special flavour treat.

Preheat the oven to 180°C/350°F/gas mark 4.

Heat the oil in a frying pan, add the aubergine slices and fry for 4–5 minutes over a high heat until softened. Add the onion slices and cook for a further 2–3 minutes.

In the meantime, place the muffin halves onto a baking tray, then smooth over the tomato purée, about ½ tablespoon per half. Bake in the oven for 8–10 minutes until the edges are golden and crisp.

Remove the muffin bases from the oven and load over the hot aubergine and onion slices. Scatter with the basil leaves and season to taste with sea salt and black pepper.

TIPS
You'll find tubes or cans of tomato purée with herbs in supermarkets. The addition of herbs gives added flavour with minimal effort on your behalf. If you have only plain tomato purée available, simply sprinkle over a pinch of dried oregano.

Garlic mushrooms on toast with dill yogurt

SERVES 2

1 tbsp sunflower oil

20 whole **button mushrooms**, brushed clean

2 **garlic** cloves, thinly sliced

2 thick slices of seeded **sourdough** bread

2 tbsp **unsweetened soya yogurt**

2 sprigs of **dill**, very finely chopped

generous pinch of sea salt and black pepper

I love this comforting lunch, which is both luxurious and simple. For me, this is perfect autumn food; it feels cosy, especially when the weather is crisp outdoors. The recipe requires very little preparation, so it can be ready in 10 minutes or so.

Heat the oil in a frying pan, add the mushrooms and cook over a medium heat for 5 minutes until softened. Add the garlic and cook for a further minute, stirring frequently to avoid sticking.

In the meantime, toast the slices of sourdough until golden, and mix together the yogurt and dill in a small bowl.

Season the garlic mushrooms with sea salt and plenty of black pepper, then spoon them on top of the toast. Dollop the dill yogurt over the mushrooms, and scatter over some extra roughly chopped dill to garnish, if you like.

TIPS

Whole button mushrooms have a wonderful texture and bite when served on toast, but if you're using larger mushrooms, such as chestnut (cremini), quarter them instead of slicing for a chunky texture.

Balsamic Mediterranean hot baguettes

SERVES 2

8 **cherry tomatoes**

———

1 medium **courgette (zucchini)**,
roughly chopped

———

1 **red onion**, thickly sliced

———

2 tbsp **balsamic vinegar**

———

2 medium **baguettes**

———

Could there be a more satisfying lunch than crusty baguettes loaded with hot, Mediterranean-style vegetables? Serve with a fresh green salad or a few homemade oven chips (page 121).

Preheat the oven to 200°C/400°F/gas mark 6.

In a bowl, combine the tomatoes, courgette and red onion. Drizzle in the balsamic vinegar and stir to coat all of the vegetables. Spoon the coated vegetables onto a baking tray and roast in the oven for 20–25 minutes until softened.

For the final 2 minutes of roasting time, put the baguettes into the oven to warm up. Remove from the oven and split them lengthways.

Carefully remove the roasted vegetables from the oven and stuff into the baguettes. Serve hot.

Pictured overleaf

TIPS
I love the combination of tomatoes, courgette and red onion, but throw in mushrooms, aubergine (eggplant) or butternut squash for seasonal variation.

Greek salad stuffed pittas

SERVES 2

6 green pitted **olives**, halved

———

½ punnet of **cherry tomatoes**, quartered

———

½ small **red onion**, finely chopped

———

1 tbsp **unsweetened soya yogurt**, chilled

———

generous pinch of sea salt and black pepper

———

2 large white **pitta** breads, toasted

———

Stuff toasted, steamy pitta breads with this creamy Greek salad. Keep the soya yogurt chilled before using, for a cooling contrast and a taste of the Mediterranean in every bite.

In a mixing bowl, stir together the olives, tomatoes and red onion. Swirl through the soya yogurt and season to taste with sea salt and black pepper.

Carefully cut or break open the toasted pittas and generously spoon in the salad. Serve while the pitta breads are still hot.

Pictured overleaf

TIPS
I love the flavour of toasted, plain pitta breads, but wholemeal and seeded are suitable alternatives.

Spicy bean and avocado wraps

SERVES 4

1 tbsp sunflower oil

1 **red onion**, thinly sliced

400g canned **red kidney beans**, drained and rinsed

1 tsp **Cajun seasoning**

4 soft **tortilla** wraps

1 **avocado**, peeled, stoned and sliced

Try these speedy and spicy wraps for lunch, with cooling strips of avocado. Feel free to throw in crisp lettuce, coriander (cilantro) or grated vegan cheese if you want to take them up a notch.

Heat the oil in a wok over a medium heat, add the red onion and cook for 2–3 minutes until softened. Add the kidney beans and Cajun seasoning and stir-fry for another 2–3 minutes until the onion and the beans are coated.

Lay out the wraps and arrange a few slices of avocado on each in a line down the centre. Spoon the spicy beans on top of the avocado, sprinkle with a little more Cajun seasoning, if you like, then fold each side inwards and roll up the wrap to envelop the filling. Enjoy hot or cold.

Mediterranean briam

SERVES 4

Suitable for freezing

4 **baking potatoes**, peeled
and thickly sliced into rounds

2 large **courgettes (zucchini)**,
thickly sliced into rounds

1 large **red onion**, sliced
into rounds

1 tsp dried **oregano**

500g (1lb 2oz) **passata**
with herbs

generous pinch of sea salt
and black pepper

**This traditional Greek baked gratin makes the perfect
lunch, served with crusty bread and a few marinated
olives. I love to make it the evening before and serve the
next day, either hot or chilled.**

Preheat the oven to 180°C/350°F/gas mark 4.

In a baking dish, arrange mixed circles or layers of sliced
potatoes, courgettes and red onion. Sprinkle with the
oregano and pour over the passata. Cover the dish loosely
with foil, then bake in the oven for 1 hour.

Remove from the oven and carefully lift off the foil.
Return to the oven for 15 minutes until the top is slightly
crisp. Season with a pinch of sea salt and black pepper.

TIPS
Adapt the recipe by switching the courgettes for sliced
aubergine (eggplant), for a seasonal variation.

Santorini tomato fritters

3 tbsp **plain (all-purpose) flour**

1 tsp **baking powder**

1 tsp dried **oregano**

300g (10oz) **cherry tomatoes**, roughly chopped

handful of **flat-leaf parsley**, finely chopped

pinch of sea salt and black pepper

4 tbsp sunflower oil

If you've been lucky enough to visit a Greek island, it's likely that you've sampled authentic tomato fritters, originating from the beautiful island of Santorini. Some varieties contain fresh mint or basil, but I love the burst of flavour that flat-leaf parsley adds. Serve hot with cool unsweetened soya yogurt to dip, and a wedge of lemon to squeeze over – perfect with a leafy green salad.

In a mixing bowl, stir together the flour, baking powder and dried oregano.

Stir in the tomatoes and flat-leaf parsley, then season with sea salt and black pepper. Add 50ml (2fl oz) cold water and stir to form a thick batter.

Heat the oil in a frying pan until hot. Add in tablespoons of the batter (up to four at a time, to avoid the fritters touching and merging) and cook for 1 minute until golden and crisp, then carefully flip the fritters and cook on the other side. Drain on paper towels or a clean dish towel, then repeat the cooking process until all of the batter has been used. Serve hot.

TIPS

The key to perfect fritters is hot oil: if the oil isn't hot enough, the fritters will be soggy. Test the oil by dropping a small amount of the mixture into the pan; if it turns golden within a few seconds, the oil is ready.

Heritage tomato bruschetta

SERVES 4

300g (10oz) mixed-colour **baby tomatoes**, quartered

4 tbsp good-quality extra virgin olive oil

⎯⎯⎯⎯

generous pinch of sea salt and black pepper

⎯⎯⎯⎯

1 **garlic** clove, halved

⎯⎯⎯⎯

1 white **baguette**, cut into 1cm (½in) thick slices

⎯⎯⎯⎯

small handful of **basil** leaves, roughly torn if large

⎯⎯⎯⎯

Bruschetta is all about using the freshest ingredients, which is why I wait until the summertime to find the best baby tomatoes, of all colours and varieties. Flat-leaf parsley or garden mint make delicious alternatives to basil leaves, for colour, fragrance and extra freshness.

In a mixing bowl, stir together the baby tomatoes and oil. Season to taste with sea salt and black pepper, then allow to infuse for 10 minutes.

Rub the cut sides of the garlic over the slices of baguette, then place a dry griddle pan over a medium–high heat. Carefully place the slices onto the hot griddle and toast for 3–4 minutes until grill lines appear on the bread. Turn using tongs, then cook on the other side for 1 minute.

Lay the griddled baguette toasts on serving plates, and liberally spoon over the tomatoes. Scatter with the basil leaves just before serving.

TIPS

Store tomatoes in the fridge to extend their shelf life, but remove them from the fridge for about an hour before eating, as the flavours become enhanced at room temperature.

Grilled Bloody Mary sandwich

SERVES 1

1 tsp sunflower oil

———

2 thick slices of good-quality **white bread**

———

1 tbsp **tomato purée (paste)**

———

1 **beef tomato**, thickly sliced into rounds

———

½ **celery** stick, finely chopped

———

few drops of **Tabasco** sauce

———

generous pinch of sea salt

———

For brunch, lunch or any time that it is not socially acceptable to drink a Bloody Mary cocktail, this toasted sandwich has tomatoes, hot sauce, celery and salt – making it the perfect pick-me-up.

Rub the surface of a cold griddle pan with the oil and place over a low heat to heat up.

Spread each slice of bread with tomato purée, then lay the tomato and celery over one slice. Sprinkle with Tabasco sauce and season with sea salt. Lay the other slice of bread over to form a sandwich.

Carefully lay the sandwich in the hot griddle pan and cook for 3–4 minutes until golden, then use a slotted spatula to carefully turn the toastie. Cook for a further 3–4 minutes until golden, then remove from the pan. Slice diagonally to serve.

TIPS

Feel free to add a few drops of Worcestershire sauce in addition to, or instead of, Tabasco sauce, but do ensure it is anchovy free.

Welsh rarebit stuffed potatoes

SERVES 4

4 large **baking potatoes**, scrubbed clean and dried thoroughly

1 tbsp sunflower oil

4 tbsp vegan **cream cheese**

2 tsp **English mustard**

small bunch of **chives**, finely chopped

few drops of vegan **Worcestershire sauce** (ensure anchovy free)

generous pinch of sea salt and black pepper

Cheesy, tangy and oh-so-comforting, these stuffed potatoes are a lunch worth waiting for. I often bake the potatoes the evening before, when I already have the oven on for my evening meal, and allow them to cool overnight, ready to put together in no time for lunch. Alternatively, you could let your slow cooker do the first bake following my recipe for slow cooker jacket potatoes (page 202). Opt for vegan cream cheese rather than vegan hard cheese to get a creamier, more buttery texture.

Preheat the oven to 200°C/400°F/gas mark 6.

Pierce the potatoes with a fork a few times, then rub in the sunflower oil. Wrap each potato in foil, then bake in the oven for 1½ hours until softened.

Remove from the oven and carefully fold back the foil. Halve each potato and leave until cool enough to handle. Carefully scoop out the potato flesh from each half into a bowl, leaving about 5mm (¼in) remaining near the skin.

Mash the potato in the bowl, along with the vegan cream cheese and mustard. Stir in the chives, then load each potato skin with the filling. Place the filled halves in a roasting tin lined with baking parchment and return to the oven to bake for 20 minutes until golden on the top.

Remove from the oven and dash over the Worcestershire sauce. Season with sea salt and black pepper, garnish with a few extra chopped chives, and chive flowers when in season, if you like, and serve hot.

TIPS

Vegan Worcestershire sauce is available in supermarkets and health-food shops. Some brands contain anchovies, so always double check the label before purchasing.

Boston beans

SERVES 2 GENEROUSLY

Suitable for freezing

1 tbsp sunflower oil

————

1 large **onion**, finely diced

————

1 tsp dried **mixed herbs**

————

400g (14oz) canned
chopped tomatoes

————

1 tbsp **black treacle
(blackstrap molasses)**

————

400g (14oz) canned **haricot
beans**, drained and rinsed

————

generous pinch of black pepper

————

**Give baked beans an all-American twist! Caramelized
onion and black treacle create a sweet and smoky sauce
– perfect for dipping crusty bread into for a hearty lunch
or on toasted sourdough for brunch. Alternatively, serve
at a barbecue as a winning side dish.**

Preheat the oven to 180°C/350°F/gas mark 4.

Heat the oil in an ovenproof pan over a medium heat,
add the onion and cook for 8–10 minutes until the onion
has caramelized, stirring occasionally to avoid sticking.
Add the herbs and cook for a further minute.

Stir in the chopped tomatoes and black treacle until
combined with the onion, then pour in the beans.
Stir again to combine, then place the lid over the dish.
Transfer the pan to the oven and bake for 30 minutes.

Remove from the oven and season with black pepper
before serving.

TIPS
Sprinkle with some extra dried mixed herbs or chopped
thyme leaves before serving, if you like.

Pease pudding

MAKES 1 JAR

250g (9oz) **yellow split peas**, soaked in cold water overnight, then drained

1 **onion**, peeled and halved

1 litre (1¾ pints) hot **vegetable stock** (page 212)

generous pinch of sea salt and black pepper

I couldn't write this book without including a traditional recipe hailing from the north-east of England. Pease pudding is a comforting savoury spread, often loaded into sandwiches or smoothed onto fresh bread, either hot or cold. For me, this is a taste of home, wherever my lunchbox may be.

Add the drained soaked yellow split peas, onion and stock to a large pan and simmer for 1 hour, with the lid loosely placed over. Stir occasionally to avoid sticking.

After 1 hour, pour in 500ml (18fl oz) just-boiled water, add the sea salt and black pepper and simmer for a further 30 minutes with the lid off.

Ladle the softened peas into a high-powered jug blender or food processor (or use a hand blender), along with any remaining cooking liquid, and blitz until smooth. Spoon out into a bowl, or into a clean jar for easy fridge storage.

TIPS
Pease pudding will keep in the fridge for up to 3 days.

Sweet potato hash

Suitable for freezing

1 tbsp sunflower oil

_____

2 medium **sweet potatoes**, peeled and diced into 2cm (1in) pieces

_____

1 **red onion**, thinly sliced

_____

2 tsp **Cajun seasoning**

_____

400g (14oz) canned **red kidney beans**, drained and rinsed

_____

handful of **coriander (cilantro)**, roughly torn

_____

generous pinch of sea salt

_____

This tasty and substantial lunch is delicious eaten either hot or cold, and makes for a perfect brunch or lunch alongside creamy avocado and tortilla wraps. Drizzle with a little lime juice for extra zing and/or add a dash of Tabasco sauce for a heat boost!

Preheat the oven to 200°C/400°F/gas mark 6.

Heat the oil in an ovenproof pan over a medium heat and add the sweet potatoes. Cook for 4–5 minutes, stirring occasionally, then add the onion and Cajun seasoning and cook for a further minute.

Remove from the heat, then stir through the red kidney beans. Place the lid on the pan, then transfer it to the oven and bake for 30 minutes until the sweet potato has softened.

Carefully remove from the oven, serve up onto plates and scatter with the coriander and sea salt.

TIPS
Canned black beans or borlotti beans are a good alternative to red kidney beans in this recipe.

SUPPERS

If you're looking to create family favourites, impressive evening meals or a simple supper for two, this chapter will show you how to get the best out of just five ingredients, without sacrificing on flavour or substance!

Greens and noodles

1 tbsp sunflower oil

1 **red chilli**, deseeded and finely chopped

100g (3½oz) **sugarsnap peas**, trimmed and sliced on the diagonal

6 large leaves of **cavolo nero**, stems removed, roughly chopped

300g (10oz) ready-to-wok soft **noodles** (ensure egg free)

juice of 1 unwaxed **lime**

generous pinch of sea salt

These simple, zingy noodles make the perfect side dish to sticky marmalade tofu (page 94) or as a light main dish when served alone. Whip up in less than 10 minutes for a quick meal when you need it most.

Heat the oil in a wok over a high heat, then add in the chilli flakes and allow to infuse for a minute.

Throw in the sugarsnap peas and cavolo nero, then stir-fry for 3–4 minutes.

Add the soft noodles to a bowl and pour over a little boiling water. Use a fork to separate the noodles, then drain away the water and add the noodles to the wok. Stir-fry for 2 minutes.

Remove the wok from the heat and stir through the lime juice. Season with sea salt just before serving.

TIPS

Substitute 1 tablespoon of light soy sauce for the sea salt to deepen the finished flavour.

Sticky marmalade tofu

SERVES 2 GENEROUSLY

390g (13½oz) block of firm **tofu**

2 tsp **plain (all-purpose) flour**

1 tbsp sunflower oil

3 heaped tbsp orange **marmalade**

pinch of dried **chilli flakes**

small handful of **coriander (cilantro)**, roughly torn

generous pinch of sea salt

During my years as a vegan, I've had a love/hate relationship with tofu. The love part is when tofu is crisp, golden and full of flavour; the hate part is when tofu is spongy and soggy! The trick to perfect tofu is to remove as much moisture as possible (I've detailed how to press it below) and gently dust it with flour before cooking, for fail-safe crisp tofu. The sticky marmalade glaze has a hint of chilli – don't miss the coriander and sea salt, which will balance and enhance all the flavours. Serve with my 5-minute fried rice (page 192), if you like.

Remove as much moisture from the tofu as possible using a tofu press. Alternatively, wrap the tofu block in paper towels and place on a plate. Place another plate on top of the block and add a couple of books or a pan to weight it down. Press for at least 1 hour.

Slice through the tofu lengthways to create three thin blocks of tofu, then chop each slice into even triangles.

Spread out the flour on a clean work surface and lightly toss each piece of tofu in the flour to coat.

Heat the oil in a large frying pan. Once the oil is hot, use tongs to add the tofu to the pan and cook for 5 minutes until golden, then turn the tofu over and cook for another 5 minutes, or until the outer is crisp and golden.

In the meantime, whisk together the marmalade, chilli flakes and 1 tablespoon of cold water in a bowl. Pour the glaze into the pan, coating the tofu evenly.

Remove from the heat and scatter with the coriander and sea salt.

TIPS
Cut out the pressing stage by sourcing pre-pressed tofu. Standard firm tofu is now available in supermarkets.

Harissa-yogurt whole roasted cauliflower with pomegranate and pistachios

SERVES 4

1 tbsp sunflower oil

8 heaped tbsp **unsweetened soya yogurt**

1 tbsp **rose harissa paste**

1 large **cauliflower**, tough stem and leaves removed

seeds from 1 ripe **pomegranate**

2 tbsp shelled **pistachios**, roughly chopped

generous pinch of sea salt and black pepper

Turn the ordinary into the extraordinary with this golden, jewelled roasted cauliflower. This is the perfect way to impress a crowd, with minimal effort on your behalf. Rose harissa infuses the yogurt with chillies and a subtle hint of sweet rose, and is a wonderful addition to your pantry. I like to serve this with citrus tabbouleh (page 182), roasted vegetables or a leafy green salad.

Preheat the oven to 200°C/400°F/gas mark 6.

In a large bowl, mix together the sunflower oil, yogurt and rose harissa paste until combined.

Dip the whole cauliflower into the yogurt mix, turning to coat all surfaces, including the sides and the base.

Place the coated cauliflower in a roasting tin or ovenproof casserole dish, then spoon over any remaining yogurt mix. Cover with a sheet of foil or a lid and bake in the oven for 45 minutes.

After 45 minutes, carefully remove the foil or lid and bake for a further 15 minutes until golden brown.

Remove from the oven and scatter over the pomegranate seeds and chopped pistachios. Season generously with sea salt and black pepper and serve hot.

TIPS

For an impressive Sunday lunch, simply add 300g (10oz) canned chopped tomatoes, 300g (10oz) canned chickpeas (garbanzo beans), drained and rinsed, and 1 teaspoon of rose harissa paste to the base of the tin or dish for the final 15 minutes of cooking time.

Indian naan fajitas

SERVES 2

1 tbsp sunflower oil

————

2 **red (bell) peppers**, deseeded and thinly sliced

————

1 **red onion**, thinly sliced

————

1 tsp **garam masala**

————

juice of ½ unwaxed **lime**

————

pinch of sea salt

————

2 large **naan** breads (ensure dairy free)

————

This recipe came about when my store cupboard was running low – and I just fancied fajitas for dinner. With no tortilla wraps or Cajun seasoning available, I decided to give fajitas an Indian twist by using naan breads, garam masala and some simple vegetables. When life gives you lemons...

Preheat the oven to 180°C/350°F/gas mark 4.

Heat the oil in a wok and throw in the peppers and onion. Stir-fry over a high heat for 5 minutes. Sprinkle over the garam masala and stir-fry for a further minute. Remove from the heat and stir through the lime juice, then season with sea salt.

Cut each large naan bread in half and sprinkle with a little water. Heat in the oven for 2–3 minutes, or according to the instructions on the packet.

Remove from the oven, spoon the spicy vegetable mixture onto each naan half, then fold to create a fajita. Squeeze over a little extra lime juice, if you like, and serve hot.

TIPS

Shop-bought naan breads can contain dairy yogurt, but 'accidentally vegan' options are available in supermarkets, so do read the label before you buy. My favourite brand make large naan breads, ideal to halve and use as two fajitas; if your naan breads are smaller, consider using four for this recipe. Garlic and coriander (cilantro) naans pack in extra flavour!

Coconut dhal

SERVES 4

Suitable for freezing

250g (9oz) dried **red lentils**, rinsed in cold water

———————

1 litre (1¾ pints) hot **vegetable stock** (page 212)

———————

2 tbsp good-quality medium **curry paste** (ensure dairy free)

———————

400ml (14fl oz) canned **coconut milk**

———————

zest and juice of 1 unwaxed **lime**

———————

pinch of black pepper

———————

This fuss-free dhal is simple to prepare, and delicious enough for the whole family to enjoy. Use this as a simple base – try adding grated carrot, courgette (zucchini), sliced red chillies or a handful of coriander (cilantro) leaves for endless dhal variations.

Put the red lentils, vegetable stock and curry paste into a large pan and bring to a gentle boil. Reduce the heat and simmer for 25–30 minutes, stirring often, until the stock has almost been fully absorbed.

Pour in the coconut milk, stir and simmer for a further 10 minutes.

Remove from the heat and stir through the lime zest and juice and black pepper.

Pictured overleaf

TIPS
Top with quick-pickled onions (page 214) and serve with my speedy chickpea masala (opposite) and generous amounts of pilau rice (page 193) for an Indian feast.

Speedy chickpea masala

SERVES 2 GENEROUSLY

Suitable for freezing

1 tbsp sunflower oil

———

1 **onion**, diced

———

2 **garlic** cloves, crushed

———

2 tbsp medium **curry paste**
(ensure dairy free)

———

400g (14oz) canned
chopped tomatoes

———

400g (14oz) canned
chickpeas (garbanzo beans),
drained and rinsed

———

generous pinch of sea salt
and black pepper

———

A classic midweek meal that is ready in 15 minutes. I love to make this masala when the store cupboard is running low, but feel free to throw in spinach, green beans or grated carrot if you have any available.

Heat the oil in a large pan, add the onion and cook over a medium heat for about 5 minutes until the onion is softened but not browned. Add in the garlic and cook for a further minute.

Stir in the curry paste until the onion and garlic is coated, then pour in the chopped tomatoes and chickpeas. Stir to combine, then allow to simmer for 10–12 minutes.

Remove from the heat and season with sea salt and black pepper to taste.

Pictured overleaf

TIPS

For an extra flourish and layer of flavour, finish with the juice of ½ unwaxed lemon and a scattering of flat-leaf parsley.

Coconut and squash traybake

SERVES 4

1 medium **butternut squash**, peeled, deseeded and cut into 3cm (1in) cubes (about 500g/ 1lb 2oz prepared weight)

handful of **green beans**, trimmed

200g (7oz) **basmati rice**

400ml (14fl oz) canned full-fat **coconut milk**

1 tbsp mild **curry paste** (ensure dairy free)

generous pinch of sea salt

Sometimes dinner is as easy as adding everything to a roasting tin and letting the oven do all the hard work. This simple traybake will be ready to serve in less than 45 minutes. I love serving it with wedges of lemon for a fresh contrast to the coconut milk.

Preheat the oven to 180°C/350°F/gas mark 4.

Arrange the butternut squash and green beans in a deep roasting tin and scatter in the rice.

In a jug, mix 200ml (7fl oz) cold water with the coconut milk and curry paste until combined. Pour this into the roasting tin, making sure it covers all of the ingredients. Cover with foil, then bake in the oven for 40–45 minutes until the squash is tender.

Remove from the oven and carefully lift off the foil. Season with sea salt before serving.

TIPS

This recipe also works well with frozen butternut squash, saving you peeling and chopping time. Frozen butternut squash is available from most supermarkets, and is a useful addition to your freezer.

Sausage, sage and bean casserole

SERVES 4

1 tbsp sunflower oil

1 **onion**, finely diced

1 tsp dried **sage**

400g (14oz) canned **chopped tomatoes**

400g (14oz) canned **haricot beans**, drained and rinsed

6 frozen vegan **sausages**

pinch of sea salt
and black pepper

I love serving this casserole family-style, with the pot in the centre of the table for everyone to tuck into – it's a real crowd-pleaser! Vegan Cumberland sausages work best in this casserole (and are readily available in supermarkets), but feel free to use your favourite vegan sausages. Serve with colcannon mash (page 201) or crusty bread for a comforting yet simple supper.

Preheat the oven to 200°C/400°F/gas mark 6.

Heat the oil in an ovenproof casserole dish, add the onion and sage and cook over a medium heat until the onion has softened but not browned.

Pour in the chopped tomatoes along with the haricot beans and stir to combine. Remove the casserole from the heat, nestle the vegan sausages into the bean and tomato mixture and cover with a lid. Bake in the oven for 30 minutes.

Carefully remove from the oven and season to taste with sea salt and black pepper before serving.

TIPS
Throw in some apple slices just before you pop the dish in the oven, if you like, for the perfect flavour partnership.

Twice-baked pumpkin and sage macaroni

SERVES 4

1 medium **pumpkin**, peeled, deseeded and chopped into rough wedges (about 500g/ 1lb 2oz prepared weight)

———

1 **onion**, quartered

———

drizzle of olive oil

———

1 tsp dried **sage**

———

500ml (18fl oz) hot **vegetable stock** (page 212)

———

300g (10oz) dried **macaroni** (ensure egg free)

———

generous pinch of sea salt and black pepper

———

If any dish represents autumn, it's this comforting pasta bake. Celebrate the season's finest produce, baked with that store-cupboard essential macaroni, for a nostalgic taste of home. If you don't have a pumpkin available, butternut squash makes a great alternative.

Preheat the oven to 200°C/400°F/gas mark 6.

Arrange the pumpkin wedges and onion quarters in a roasting tin, then drizzle with the olive oil. Roast in the oven for 30–35 minutes until the pumpkin has softened.

Remove the roasted pumpkin and onion from the oven and place in a high-powered jug blender. Scatter in the sage, then pour in the hot stock. Blitz until completely smooth. (If you're using a hand blender, add the ingredients to a large bowl and keep blitzing until smooth.)

Arrange the macaroni in a large ovenproof dish, then pour over the pumpkin purée, stirring to ensure all the pieces of pasta are covered.

Cover the dish with foil and bake in the oven for 30–35 minutes until the pasta is tender but still with some bite. Season with sea salt and black pepper and serve hot.

TIPS
Most dried pasta in supermarkets is egg free, but always check the label before you buy.

Gnocchi arrabiata

SERVES 2

500g (1lb 2oz) **gnocchi**
(ensure egg free)

1 tbsp sunflower oil

½ tsp dried **chilli flakes**

2 **garlic** cloves, crushed

500g (1lb 2oz) **passata**

1 tsp **caster (superfine) sugar**

generous pinch of sea salt
and black pepper

Shop-bought potato gnocchi is an essential for any store cupboard, as you can have a comforting bowl of fluffy potato dumplings within minutes. In this dish, I combine a classic chilli-infused sauce with gnocchi – simply reduce the chilli flakes to ¼ teaspoon for a less feisty arrabiata sauce. Serve with steamed green beans, or a leafy green salad, if you like.

Add the gnocchi to a large pan of simmering water and cook for 8–10 minutes until fluffy, or according to the packet instructions.

In the meantime, add the sunflower oil and chilli flakes to a separate pan and cook over a medium heat for 2 minutes. Add the garlic and cook for a further minute.

Stir in the passata and add the sugar, which will take away the acidity of the tomato passata. Reduce the heat to low-medium and cook for 10 minutes, stirring frequently.

Drain the gnocchi thoroughly, then add to the arrabiata sauce and stir though to coat the gnocchi.

Season with sea salt and black pepper to taste. Serve hot.

TIPS
For extra colour and a fresh flavour, scatter with chopped flat-leaf parsley just before serving.

Roasted broccoli rigatoni

200g (7oz) **Tenderstem broccoli**, any very tough stem ends discarded

1 tbsp good-quality olive oil, plus extra to finish

½ tsp dried **chilli flakes**

2 **garlic** cloves, thinly sliced

150g (5oz) dried **rigatoni** (ensure egg free)

zest and juice of 1 unwaxed **lemon**, plus some lemon slice to serve

generous pinch of sea salt and black pepper

Roasting broccoli takes the humble vegetable to new flavour levels. I love Tenderstem broccoli as it is easy to use, with minimal preparation – it also cooks in no time! Combine with a hint of chilli, garlic and lemon for a satisfying bowl of pasta.

Preheat the oven to 200°C/400°F/gas mark 6.

Arrange the broccoli evenly on a baking tray, then drizzle over the olive oil. Scatter over the chilli flakes and garlic slices, then roast in the oven for 10 minutes until the broccoli appears golden at the edges and slightly crisp.

In the meantime, bring a pan of water to the boil and cook the pasta for 8–10 minutes until *al dente*. Remove from the heat and drain thoroughly.

Carefully spoon the roasted broccoli, chilli flakes and garlic slices over the pasta, along with any hot oil from the tray. Drizzle with a little extra olive oil, sprinkle with the lemon zest and squeeze over the lemon juice. Stir through.

Season generously with sea salt and black pepper and serve with a few lemon slices for squeezing over.

TIPS

I love the way the olive oil, chilli and lemon catches inside the rigatoni tubes, but any egg-free pasta you like will be just as delicious. Most dried pasta found in the supermarkets is simply made from semolina flour, but always check the label before you buy.

Smoky ratatouille

SERVES 4

Suitable for freezing

1 tbsp sunflower oil

———

1 **red onion**, roughly chopped

———

2 medium **courgettes (zucchini)**, roughly chopped

———

1 **red (bell) pepper**, deseeded and roughly chopped

———

300ml (10fl oz) **versatile tomato sauce** (page 207); store-bought is also fine

———

1 tsp **smoked paprika**

———

pinch of smoked sea salt and black pepper

———

I love a bowl of fresh ratatouille on cooler summer evenings, served with crusty bread (for dipping), and a glass of cider. Take the love of ratatouille into autumn with a smokier version of the classic dish. If I'm feeling particularly hungry, I like to add 400g (14oz) canned butter (lima) beans that have been drained and rinsed.

Heat the sunflower oil in a large pan, add the red onion and cook over a medium heat for 2–3 minutes until the onion begins to soften. Then add the courgettes and red pepper and cook for 10 minutes, stirring frequently.

Pour in the tomato sauce and 100ml (3½fl oz) cold water. Stir in the smoked paprika, then simmer over a low heat for 20 minutes.

Remove from the heat and season to taste with smoked sea salt and black pepper.

TIPS

If you don't have any versatile tomato sauce (page 207) to hand, add a crushed garlic clove to the courgettes and pepper, along with 1 teaspoon of dried basil and 400g (14oz) canned chopped tomatoes.

Simple Bolognese

SERVES 4

Suitable for freezing

1 tbsp sunflower oil

⎯⎯⎯

2 **onions**, finely diced

⎯⎯⎯

2 **carrots**, peeled and finely diced

⎯⎯⎯

2 **garlic** cloves, crushed

⎯⎯⎯

300ml (10fl oz) **versatile tomato sauce** (page 207); store-bought is also fine

⎯⎯⎯

400g (14oz) canned **green lentils**, drained and rinsed

⎯⎯⎯

generous pinch of sea salt and black pepper

⎯⎯⎯

It's good to have a recipe that you can turn to again and again. For me, it's this simple and fuss-free Bolognese. Don't be fooled into thinking a good Bolognese needs a long list of ingredients; simplicity is beautiful here. The key to packing in flavour is to let the onions brown gently – the caramelized result is delicious! I like to serve this with egg-free spaghetti and a leafy salad.

Heat the sunflower oil in a large pan, add the onions and cook over a medium heat for 8–10 minutes, stirring occasionally, until golden brown.

Add the carrots and garlic and cook for a further minute.

Pour in the tomato sauce and green lentils along with 200ml (7fl oz) cold water, then reduce the heat to low-medium. Simmer for 30–35 minutes with the pan lid loosely placed over, stirring frequently to avoid sticking, until the carrots have softened.

Remove the pan from the heat and season with sea salt and black pepper to taste.

TIPS

Scatter over some basil leaves if you have them available, for added flavour and fragrance.

Pear and butter bean traybake

SERVES 2

2 Conference **pears**, halved and cored

6 mixed-colour baby **carrots**, scrubbed and halved lengthways

12 **new potatoes**, washed

½ tsp dried **sage**

2 tbsp sunflower oil

400g (14oz) canned **butter (lima) beans**, drained and rinsed

generous pinch of sea salt and black pepper

Throw together this all-in-one traybake for a satisfying, simple supper. Pears offer a sweet, melt-in-the-mouth flavour alongside earthy new potatoes and butter beans. I love the woody taste of sage in this recipe, but rosemary works equally well.

Preheat the oven to 200°C/400°F/gas mark 6.

Arrange the pears, carrots and new potatoes in a roasting tin, then scatter with the dried sage. Drizzle with the sunflower oil and roast in the oven for 30 minutes.

Carefully remove the tin from the oven and add the butter beans evenly across the tin. Reduce the oven temperature to 180°C/350°F/gas mark 4 and bake for a further 10 minutes.

Season generously with sea salt and black pepper just before serving.

TIPS

If you can't get hold of baby carrots, use two ordinary carrots, peeled and roughly chopped. This recipe is delicious served with mushroom gravy (page 211), which brings the sweet and earthy flavours together.

Leek and mushroom pot pies

SERVES 2

1 tbsp sunflower oil

1 medium **leek**, finely chopped

250g (9oz) **chestnut (cremini) mushrooms**, brushed clean and roughly sliced

2 **garlic** cloves, crushed

5 tbsp **soya single cream**

generous pinch of sea salt and black pepper

1 sheet of ready-rolled **puff pastry** (ensure dairy free)

These cosy pies are creamy, fragrant and satisfying. I love serving them as small individual portions, but feel free to create one large pie to share, family-style. Many brands of shop-bought puff pastry are made with vegetable oil instead of butter, making it accidentally vegan (but do check the ingredients before you buy).

Preheat the oven to 200°C/400°F/gas mark 6.

Heat the oil in a frying pan, add the leek and soften over a medium heat for 4–5 minutes. Throw in the mushrooms and cook for a further 5 minutes, stirring occasionally.

Add the garlic and cook for 2 minutes until softened and fragrant. Then pour in the soya single cream and cook for a further minute. Season with sea salt and black pepper to taste and remove from the heat.

Unroll the puff pastry sheet. Position two small pie dishes upside down on the pastry and use a knife to cut out around them. If you like, you can use the excess pastry to cut out shapes to decorate the pie tops.

Fill the pie dishes with the creamy leek and mushrooms, then place the pastry discs over the top, crimping the edges all the way round with a fork. Bake in the oven for 15–18 minutes until golden.

Pictured overleaf

TIPS
For a golden finish to the pastry, brush with a little soya milk before baking.

Homemade oven chips

SERVES 4

4 large **King Edward potatoes**
(or any other type of fluffy
baking potato), peeled and cut
into 2cm (1in) thick chips

2 tbsp sunflower oil

few sprinkles of **malt vinegar**

generous pinch of sea salt

**Golden and crisp on the outside and fluffy on the inside,
these homemade oven chips are simple to create and
delicious to eat. No need to bring out the deep fryer!**

**Serve with leek and mushroom pot pies (opposite),
or between two thick slices of white bread.**

Preheat the oven to 200°C/400°F/gas mark 6.

Rinse the chipped potatoes under cold water and pat dry
with a clean dish towel, to remove the excess starch.

Lay the chipped potatoes on a baking tray in an even layer
(use two tins if necessary to avoid overcrowding). Drizzle
with the sunflower oil, then bake in the oven for 45–50
minutes until golden and crisp.

Remove from the oven and sprinkle with the malt vinegar
and sea salt flakes. Serve hot.

Pictured overleaf

Pappardelle with creamy white wine mushrooms

SERVES 2

1 tbsp sunflower oil

250g (9oz) **chestnut (cremini) mushrooms**, brushed clean and roughly sliced

3 **garlic** cloves, crushed

generous glug of **white wine** (ensure vegan)

160g (5½oz) dried **pappardelle** (ensure egg free)

200ml (7fl oz) **soya single cream**

generous pinch of sea salt and black pepper

One of life's true pleasures is a big bowl of slippery pappardelle pasta, with a creamy, garlicky sauce. White wine brings a touch of acidity to the earthy mushrooms, but do check it is vegan friendly, as some wines contain animal ingredients. Pull on your cosiest sweater, put your feet up and melt into this bowl of heaven.

Heat the oil in a large frying pan, add the mushrooms and cook over a medium heat for 8-10 minutes until softened and fragrant. Add the garlic and cook for a further minute. Pour in the white wine and reduce for 4-5 minutes.

Meanwhile, bring a large pan of water to the boil and cook the pappardelle for 8-10 minutes until *al dente*.

Pour the soya cream over the mushrooms and stir. Reduce the heat to low-medium and simmer gently for 5 minutes, stirring frequently. Season generously with sea salt and black pepper.

Drain the pappardelle thoroughly, then use tongs to transfer the pasta to the pan of sauce. Coat all of the pasta in the creamy sauce, then serve.

TIPS

Pappardelle is a thick ribbon pasta, perfect to hold a creamy sauce. Dried pappardelle is often made without eggs, but always check the ingredients before buying. You'll find it in supermarkets or Mediterranean delis.

Roasted cherry tomato risotto

SERVES 4

300g (10oz) **cherry tomatoes**

2 tbsp sunflower oil

2 **garlic** cloves, crushed

250g (9oz) **Arborio risotto rice**

500g (1lb 2oz) **passata**

800ml (28fl oz) hot **vegetable stock** (page 212)

generous pinch of sea salt and black pepper

For me, this recipe is risotto perfection. Creamy Arborio rice, a hint of garlic and sweet roasted cherry tomatoes – and what's more, it's ready in just 30 minutes. Serve in warmed bowls.

Preheat the oven to 180°C/350°F/gas mark 4.

Arrange the cherry tomatoes on a baking tray and drizzle with 1 tablespoon of the oil. Roast in the oven for 20–25 minutes.

Meanwhile, prepare the risotto. Heat the remaining oil in a large pan, add the garlic and cook over a medium heat for 1 minute until the garlic has softened and infused the oil. Pour in the rice and cook for a further minute until the edges of the rice have become transparent.

Pour the passata into a large bowl or jug and mix in the vegetable stock until combined. Ladle or pour a quarter of the passata–stock liquid into the pan, stirring frequently. Allow the rice to swell and cook, then add in another quarter of the liquid. Continue until all of the liquid has been used and absorbed; this should take 25–30 minutes. Remove from the heat.

Remove the roasted cherry tomatoes from the oven, then stir them through the risotto. Season with sea salt and plenty of black pepper to taste. Serve hot.

TIPS
Scatter over some basil leaves if you have them available, for added flavour and fragrance.

Beetroot, onion and thyme galette

SERVES 4

1 sheet of ready-rolled **puff pastry** (ensure dairy free)

————

1 tbsp sunflower oil

————

1 **onion**, thinly sliced into rings

————

½ tsp **thyme** leaves, finely chopped

————

300g (10oz) vacuum-packed cooked **beetroot** (about 3 small beetroots), drained of excess juice and thinly sliced

————

zest and juice of ¼ unwaxed **lemon**

————

generous pinch of sea salt

————

This cheat's galette has the pastry base cooked separately to the topping, for fail-safe results every time (no soggy bottom on this pastry!). Assemble the galette just before serving to ensure the base remains crisp. Pre-cooked beetroot is a fuss-free way of preparing and enjoying the vegetable, which is delicious with thyme and lemon.

Preheat the oven to 220°C/425°F/gas mark 7.

Unroll the pastry onto a baking tray and roughly fold in the corners and edges to form a 2cm (1in) border. Use a fork to prick all over the centre of the pastry, then bake in the oven for 12–15 minutes until golden.

Meanwhile, heat the oil in a frying pan, add the onion and cook over a medium–high heat for 4–5 minutes until softened. Scatter in the thyme leaves and cook for a further minute.

Carefully add the sliced beetroot to the pan and gently fry for 4–5 minutes, without breaking up the slices. Remove from the heat and squeeze over the lemon juice.

Remove the pastry from the oven, and carefully arrange the beetroot topping over the top. Scatter with the lemon zest and season with sea salt before serving.

TIPS
Many brands of shop-bought puff pastry are dairy-free, using vegetable fats instead of butter, but do check the ingredients list before you buy.

Parsnip and chickpea tagine

SERVES 4

Suitable for freezing

1 tbsp sunflower oil

2 **red onions**, roughly chopped

4 **parsnips**, peeled and quartered lengthways

1 tsp **ras el hanout**

400g (14oz) canned **chickpeas (garbanzo beans)**, drained and rinsed

400g (14oz) canned **chopped tomatoes**

generous pinch of sea salt and black pepper

I've often skipped past tagine recipes due to the long, complicated ingredients lists; however, with a few short cuts, this tagine is simple to prepare yet still very tasty. Fragrant parsnips and sweet red onions flavour the chickpeas, along with ras el hanout, a blend of Moroccan spices traditionally used in tagines. Ras el hanout often contains ground cumin seeds, cinnamon, ginger, coriander and rose petals – packing a flavour punch in one easy step. You'll find this spice blend available in most supermarkets, in the dried herbs and spices aisle.

Preheat the oven to 180°C/350°F/gas mark 4.

Heat the oil in an ovenproof casserole dish, add the onions and parsnips and cook over a medium-high heat for 4-5 minutes, stirring frequently. Sprinkle over the ras el hanout and cook for a further minute.

Remove from the heat and pour in the chickpeas and chopped tomatoes, along with 200ml (7fl oz) cold water. Stir to coat the vegetables, then cover the casserole with a lid and cook in the oven for 30 minutes until the parsnips have softened.

Carefully remove from the oven. Season with sea salt and black pepper to taste.

TIPS
Squeeze over the juice of half an unwaxed lemon and scatter with mint leaves or flat-leaf parsley for freshness, if you have them available. This is delicious served with baba ganoush (page 189) and flatbreads on the side.

Chunky chilli

Suitable for freezing

1 tbsp sunflower oil

2 medium **sweet potatoes**, peeled and chopped into even chunks

1 **yellow (bell) pepper**, deseeded and roughly chopped

2 tsp mild **chilli powder**

400g (14oz) canned **kidney beans**, drained and rinsed

400g (14oz) canned **chopped tomatoes**

pinch of smoked sea salt

For a family-friendly, one-pot dinner, whip up this sweet potato chilli. Feel free to adjust the quantity of chilli powder to taste (this recipe creates a mild chilli). Serve with rice, tortilla chips or corn on the cob.

Heat the oil in a large pan, add the sweet potato and yellow pepper and cook over a medium heat for 5 minutes until the sweet potato begins to soften. Stir in the chilli powder to coat the vegetables.

Pour in the kidney beans and chopped tomatoes, then reduce the heat to low–medium. Simmer for 25 minutes until the sweet potato has completely softened.

Remove from the heat and season with smoked sea salt to taste before serving.

TIPS

Top with coriander (cilantro) and/or chopped spring onions (scallions), if you like, for a pop of colour and additional texture.

Baked sweet potato enchiladas

SERVES 4

Suitable for freezing

1 tbsp sunflower oil

———

2 **sweet potatoes**, peeled and chopped into 2cm (1in) chunks

———

1 **green (bell) pepper**, deseeded and diced

———

2 tsp mild **chilli powder**

———

400g (14oz) canned **chopped tomatoes**

———

pinch of smoked sea salt

———

8 soft **tortilla** wraps

———

This Mexican classic is full of authentic flavour, with sweet potatoes and green pepper. The recipe also serves as a base that you can vary by adding other ingredients, including red kidney beans, vegan cheese, onions and even grated dark chocolate (ensure it's dairy free)! I like to serve this with a sweetcorn salad (opposite).

Heat the oil in a large pan, add the sweet potatoes and green pepper and cook, stirring occasionally, over a medium heat for 5 minutes until the pepper has softened.

Stir through the chilli powder and pour in the chopped tomatoes. Bring to the boil, then simmer for 20–25 minutes until the sweet potato has started to soften.

Preheat the oven to 180°C/350°F/gas mark 4.

Remove the pan from the heat and season with smoked sea salt. Spoon out 4 tablespoons of the tomato sauce (without any sweet potato and pepper) and set aside.

Lay a tortilla wrap on a clean, flat surface and add 2 tablespoons of the hot mix in a line across the centre. Fold in the side edges and then the top and bottom edges to form a closed wrap; place it in a rectangular baking dish. Repeat for all of the wraps, pushing each one close to the next so the dish appears packed.

Drizzle the saved tomato sauce over the middle of the enchiladas, then bake in the oven for 30–35 minutes until the edges are golden.

Pictured overleaf

 TIPS

For vibrant colour and added zing, scatter over quick-pickled onions (page 214), coriander (cilantro) and a squeeze of lime just before serving.

Mexican sweetcorn salad

SERVES 2

300g (10oz) canned **sweetcorn**, drained and rinsed

1 **avocado**, peeled, stoned and evenly diced

1 **red (bell) pepper**, finely diced

2 **spring onions (scallions)**, thinly sliced

juice of 1 unwaxed **lime**

generous pinch of smoked sea salt

This colourful, crunchy and fresh salad will satisfy all of your summer cravings. So sit back, relax and pretend you're on a beach in Mexico!

Combine the sweetcorn, avocado, red pepper and spring onions in a bowl.

Squeeze over the lime juice and sprinkle with smoked sea salt. Toss and serve.

Pictured overleaf

TIPS

Frozen sweetcorn also works well in this recipe – simply defrost thoroughly before using.

Sweet potato Caribbean curry

Suitable for freezing

1 tbsp sunflower oil

4 medium **sweet potatoes**, peeled and chopped into 2cm (1in) chunks

1 **red (bell) pepper**, sliced

2 tsp **jerk seasoning**

400ml (400ml) canned full-fat **coconut milk**

handful of **coriander (cilantro)**, stalks removed

pinch of sea salt

Creamy and gently spiced, this vibrant curry will transport you to warmer climates, wherever you are. Jerk seasoning is available in supermarkets, in the dried herbs and spices aisle. This handy spice mix combines allspice, paprika, chillies, nutmeg and thyme, delivering a warm kick to curries, stews and roasted vegetables with minimal effort. Serve with Jamaican rice (opposite).

Gently heat the oil in a large pan over a medium heat, then add the sweet potato chunks and red pepper slices. Cook for 5 minutes until the sweet potato starts to soften, stirring often to prevent sticking.

Spoon over the jerk seasoning, then pour in the coconut milk. Simmer for 25 minutes, stirring occasionally, until the sweet potato is tender.

Remove the pan from the heat and scatter over the coriander. Season with sea salt to taste.

Pictured overleaf

TIPS
Throw in spinach, kale or watercress for extra colour, texture and to boost the nutritional value.

Jamaican rice

SERVES 2

180g (6oz) **basmati rice**

400g (14oz) canned **kidney beans**, drained and rinsed

2 **spring onions (scallions)**, finely chopped

handful of **flat-leaf parsley** leaves, roughly torn

juice of 1 unwaxed **lime**

generous pinch of sea salt and black pepper

Serve this rice as a side dish to my sweet potato Caribbean curry (opposite), or enjoy on its own as a warm salad. Substitute pinto beans or black beans for the kidney beans, for easy variations on this fail-safe recipe.

Place the basmati rice in a medium pan and cover with 350ml (12fl oz) cold water. Loosely place the lid on the pan and bring to the boil over a medium–high heat. Cook for 10–12 minutes until the water has been absorbed and the rice appears fluffy.

Remove from the heat and separate the grains using a fork. Stir through the kidney beans, spring onions and flat-leaf parsley until evenly distributed.

Squeeze in the lime juice and stir. Season with sea salt and black pepper to taste.

Pictured overleaf

TIPS
Basmati rice has a wonderful fragrance, which works beautifully with the lime juice. It also has the added benefit of cooking in under 15 minutes!

Black bean jambalaya

1 tbsp sunflower oil

———————

1 **green (bell) pepper**, deseeded and roughly chopped

———————

1 **red onion**, thinly sliced

———————

2 tsp **Cajun seasoning**

———————

200g (7oz) **long-grain rice**

———————

400g (14oz) canned **black beans**, drained and rinsed

———————

generous pinch of sea salt and black pepper

———————

The whole family will love this one-pot, spiced rice dish, which is delicious served hot for dinner or cold for lunch. Cajun seasoning is a pre-mixed blend of herbs and spices containing dried chillies, smoked paprika, oregano, thyme and garlic – you will find it in the spice aisle of most supermarkets. Serve with wedges of unwaxed lime for fresh and fun squeezing and tortilla chips, if you like.

Heat the oil in a large pan, add the green pepper and onion and cook over a medium heat for 3–4 minutes until softened. Stir through the Cajun seasoning to coat the vegetables, then stir through the rice.

Pour in 700ml (1¼ pints) just-boiled water and simmer for 20 minutes, stirring frequently to avoid sticking.

After 20 minutes, pour in the black beans, then simmer for a further 10 minutes until the rice has softened, again stirring frequently.

Remove from the heat and season to taste with sea salt and black pepper.

Baked aubergine with dukkah

SERVES 2

1 tbsp sunflower oil

───────

1 large **aubergine (eggplant)**, thickly sliced into rounds

───────

1 tsp dried **oregano**

───────

2 **garlic** cloves, thinly sliced

───────

500g (1lb 2oz) **passata**

───────

2 tbsp **dukkah**

───────

generous pinch of sea salt

───────

This simple supper is best served with a chunk of crusty bread and a glass of red wine, or it can be enjoyed as part of a bigger feast with easy flatbreads (page 194), cheat's ultimate houmous (page 190) and citrus tabbouleh (page 182).

Preheat the oven to 180°C/350°F/gas mark 4.

Heat the oil in a large frying pan, add the aubergine slices and oregano and cook for 4–5 minutes over a medium heat, stirring frequently, until the aubergine begins to brown. Add the garlic and cook for a further minute.

Tip the aubergine and garlic into a roasting tin or baking dish and pour over the passata. Transfer to the oven to bake for 30 minutes.

Remove the baked aubergine from the oven and scatter with the dukkah. Carefully return to the oven for a further 5 minutes for the dukkah to gently toast.

Remove from the oven and season with sea salt before slicing and serving onto plates.

TIPS

Dukkah is a blend of chopped nuts, seeds, herbs and spices used for seasoning and crunch. You can find it in large supermarkets or at Middle Eastern shops.

SWEETS

From fruity breakfasts to traditional puddings, sweet treats and summer ices, these recipes will bring happiness to everyone cooking and eating them. The hardest part is deciding what to make first!

Hot cinnamon blueberries and yogurt

SERVES 2

150g (5oz) fresh or frozen **blueberries**

zest and juice of 1 unwaxed **lemon**

1 tbsp **maple syrup**

½ tsp ground **cinnamon**

8 tbsp **vanilla soya yogurt**, chilled

What a way to start your day! Cool yogurt topped with hot cinnamon-sweetened blueberry compote is refreshing and nourishing – and it's ready in under 10 minutes.

Add the blueberries, lemon juice, maple syrup and cinnamon to a pan, then bring to a gentle simmer over a medium heat. Stir frequently, and gently press down on the blueberries, allowing the juice to colour the compote. Cook for 5–7 minutes until slightly thickened.

Spoon the chilled yogurt evenly into bowls, top with the hot cinnamon blueberries and sprinkle over the lemon zest. Dust over a little more cinnamon, if you fancy, and serve immediately.

TIPS

Vanilla-flavoured soya yogurt gives a lovely sweet contrast to the blueberries and lemon juice, but it also works well with coconut or almond yogurt.

Carrot cake porridge

80g (3oz) whole rolled **oats**

400ml (14fl oz) **sweetened almond milk**

pinch of finely grated **nutmeg**

1 large **carrot**, peeled and grated

1 tbsp **sultanas (golden raisins)**

With all of the flavours of classic carrot cake, this porridge is a dream breakfast. All of the family will love this one too. Sprinkle over a few toasted flaked almonds for extra crunch and added protein, if you like.

Put the oats, almond milk and nutmeg into a pan and simmer the porridge over a medium-high heat for 3–4 minutes, stirring frequently.

Stir through the grated carrot and sultanas and cook for a further minute.

Serve in bowls, sprinkled with a little more nutmeg, if you like, and enjoy immediately.

Apple bircher muesli

SERVES 2

100g (3½oz) whole rolled **oats**

2 tbsp blanched chopped **hazelnuts**

2 **green apples**, cut into matchsticks or grated

200ml (7fl oz) good-quality cloudy **apple juice**

1 tbsp **unsweetened soya yogurt**

Prepare this muesli the night before, refrigerate, then simply enjoy in the morning. Who said you can't have a healthy, filling breakfast before your morning commute?

Mix together the oats, hazelnuts and apples in a clean jar or bowl.

Stir in the apple juice and soya yogurt until all of the ingredients are coated. Add the lid to the jar or cover the bowl and refrigerate overnight, then enjoy for breakfast the next morning.

TIPS
Use this recipe as a base and add in extra nuts, seeds or dried fruits. Dried sour cherries are my favourite extra addition!

Lime curd

MAKES 1 SMALL JAR

zest and juice of 3 unwaxed **limes**

150g (5oz) **granulated sugar**

400ml (14fl oz) **sweetened soya milk**

1 tbsp **cornflour (cornstarch)**

1 tbsp vegan **butter**

Perfect as a cake drizzle, pudding filling or spread onto scones or into sandwiches for a picnic, this lime curd is both creamy and zesty. It's so simple to make with just store-cupboard ingredients (and without dairy or eggs).

Add the lime zest and juice, sugar, soya milk and cornflour to a pan, then bring to a simmer for 10 minutes over a medium heat. Whisk frequently until it begins to thicken.

Stir in the vegan butter and cook for a further 2 minutes until smooth.

Allow to cool a little, then pour into a clean jar. When completely cool, add the lid and chill in the fridge overnight or for a few hours until set.

TIPS
This curd will last for up to 1 week in the fridge.

Zesty bread and butter pudding

SERVES 6–8

800ml (28fl oz) **vanilla soya milk**

4 tbsp **cornflour (cornstarch)**

6 tbsp thick-cut **marmalade**

8 thick slices of **white bread**, cut diagonally into quarters

4 tbsp **sultanas (golden raisins)**

This traditional British pudding is delicious, comforting and warming on a cold winter's day. There's no need to use vegan butter on the bread, as the vanilla–marmalade custard absorbs and moistens it beautifully.

Heat the vanilla soya milk in a pan over a low–medium heat until hot but not boiling. Spoon in the cornflour and use a balloon whisk to mix until combined. Continue to cook for 8–10 minutes until thickened, whisking frequently. Stir in the marmalade and cook for a further minute.

Preheat the oven to 180°C/350°F/gas mark 4.

Arrange the quarters of bread in a deep baking dish, allowing them to overlap. Sprinkle the bread with the sultanas. Pour over the hot vanilla–marmalade custard, then leave to stand for 10 minutes to allow the bread to absorb some of the custard.

Bake in the oven for 35–40 minutes until golden and bubbling at the corners. Serve hot.

TIPS

Vanilla-flavoured soya milk can be found in most supermarkets and health-food stores.

Victoria sponge mug cake

SERVES 1
(or 2, if you're feeling particularly generous)

4 tbsp **self-raising flour**

———

2 tbsp **granulated sugar**

———

4 tbsp **vanilla soya milk**

———

1 tbsp sunflower oil

———

1 tbsp **strawberry jam**

———

For those times when you need cake in a hurry, try my speedy version of the classic British cake – cooked in a mug!

Mix together the flour and sugar in a large mug. Add the vanilla soya milk and sunflower oil, then mix until smooth.

Make a small well in the centre of the mixture, spoon in the strawberry jam and cover with the cake batter so that the jam isn't visible (this will prevent burning).

Microwave on high for 1 minute 30 seconds. Allow to cool for 2 minutes before enjoying.

TIPS

If you don't have vanilla soya milk available, use the same quantity of sweetened soya milk and add ½ teaspoon of vanilla extract.

Pretzel and popcorn fridge cake

MAKES ABOUT 8
SQUARES

250g (9oz) **dark chocolate**,
broken into even pieces
(ensure dairy free)

2 tbsp vegan **butter**
(ensure oil-based – see tip)

2 tbsp **golden syrup
(light corn syrup)**

180g (6oz) salted snack **pretzels**

generous handful (about
10g/¼oz) of **sweet popcorn**
(ensure dairy free)

**Every home cook needs a go-to fridge cake recipe – and
this is my favourite. Smooth chocolate, salted, crunchy
pretzels and light popcorn create this fridge cake of
dreams that everyone will love! I often make this the day
before I need it, refrigerate overnight to set, then slice
up just before serving.**

Place the chocolate pieces in a large heatproof bowl, then
carefully set the bowl over a pan of gently simmering
water, making sure the bottom of the bowl doesn't touch
the water. Heat the chocolate, stirring occasionally, until
melted and glossy. Add the vegan butter and golden syrup
and stir until melted and combined.

Carefully remove the bowl from the pan. Pour in the
pretzels and popcorn and stir to ensure they are
completely coated in the chocolate.

Line a small, shallow baking tin with baking parchment,
then spoon the mixture into the tin, pressing it gently to
the edges. Smooth over the top with the back of a spoon.
Refrigerate for at least 6 hours (or overnight) until firm and
set, before slicing into even squares.

TIPS

Vegan butter can have variations in the amounts of oil
and water it contains. If the butter you're using is water-
based, then it may cause the melted chocolate to seize.
Check the back of the tub to ensure the largest ingredient
in your vegan butter is oil – this will ensure a glossy and
runny chocolate sauce.

Chocolate hazelnut swirls

MAKES 12

1 sheet of ready-rolled **puff pastry** (ensure dairy free)

———————

200g (7oz) vegan **chocolate spread**

———————

2 tbsp blanched and chopped **hazelnuts**, plus extra for sprinkling

———————

Discovering that many supermarket brands of pastry are accidentally vegan due to the use of vegetable fats instead of butter (always check the ingredients before buying) has opened up a world of home-baking opportunities. I love these nutty, chocolatey pastries as a sweet snack, but I've also been known to enjoy one or two for breakfast. Vegan chocolate spreads are available in supermarkets, health-food shops and at online vegan retailers.

Preheat the oven to 220°C/425°F/gas mark 7 and line two baking trays with baking parchment.

Unroll the puff pastry sheet and spoon over the chocolate spread. Spread it liberally over the pastry, then scatter over the chopped hazelnuts.

Starting at one of the short ends of the pastry, tightly roll the pastry to the other side, to form one full roll. Slice the roll into 12 pieces and place on the baking tin.

Bake the swirls in the oven for 12–15 minutes until the pastry is golden. Sprinkle with a few more chopped hazelnuts, then serve hot or cold.

TIPS
You can find chopped hazelnuts in supermarkets, which saves chopping effort and time.

Pecan, cinnamon and banana oat bars

MAKES ABOUT 8 BARS

2 ripe **bananas**, peeled

———

1 tbsp **maple syrup**

———

200g (7oz) whole rolled **oats**

———

pinch of ground **cinnamon**

———

small handful of **pecans**,
roughly chopped

———

Bake these squidgy, oaty bars for a breakfast on the go, or a light pick-me-up in the afternoon. The riper the bananas, the sweeter the overall flavour, so feel free to leave out the maple syrup if you think the bars will be sweet enough.

Preheat the oven to 180°C/350°F/gas mark 4.

Mash the bananas into a rough paste in a bowl and stir in the maple syrup. Add the oats, cinnamon and pecans and stir again, then use your hands to fully combine.

Press tightly into a small, shallow baking tin and smooth the top with the back of a spoon. Bake in the oven for 15 minutes. Remove from the oven and slice into bars while still warm, before turning out onto a wire rack to cool completely.

 TIPS

Switch the pecans for sultanas (golden raisins), freeze-dried raspberries or dried cranberries for tasty variations (which children will love too).

Lemon and olive oil shortbread

MAKES ABOUT 10
FINGERS

200g (7oz) **plain (all-purpose) flour**

100g (3½oz) **icing (confectioner's) sugar**

zest of 1 unwaxed **lemon**, finely grated

pinch of sea salt

80ml (3fl oz) good-quality extra virgin olive oil

These crumbly slices of shortbread make the perfect biscuit to accompany a hot cup of tea. There's no need for rubbing in vegan butter here; extra virgin olive oil is an unexpected and quite excellent replacement.

Preheat the oven to 160°C/325°F/gas mark 3.

Mix together the flour, icing sugar and lemon zest in a large bowl. Stir in the sea salt.

Pour in the olive oil and stir to just combine, then use your hands to fully bring the mixture together. Don't be tempted to add any additional olive oil – the mixture should come together when you squeeze it and crumble when you let go (that's what will give it a short texture).

Press into a small, shallow baking tin, using your hands to pack the mixture tightly, then lightly prick with a fork in straight lines down the length of the pressed mixture.

Bake in the oven for 18–20 minutes until just starting to turn golden at the edges. Remove from the oven and allow to cool for 10 minutes before slicing into fingers with a sharp knife. Allow to cool fully before removing from the baking tin.

TIPS
Don't allow the shortbread to become golden in the oven – shortbread should remain pale. Just like any biscuit, it will harden as it cools.

Easiest-ever peanut butter fudge

MAKES 20 SMALL
SQUARES

180g (6oz) vegan **butter**

200g (7oz) smooth
peanut butter

1 tsp **vanilla** extract

pinch of sea salt

450g (1lb) **icing
(confectioner's) sugar**,
plus extra for dusting

**Traditional fudge needs skill, precision and a sugar
thermometer, but if you're looking for a simple, fail-safe
recipe, try this peanut butter fudge. Box up for gifts,
or treat yourself to a few squares of this moreish treat.
Who knew it could be so easy?**

Put the vegan butter and peanut butter into a large pan
and melt over a low heat, mixing gently to combine. When
it is all combined, stir in the vanilla extract and sea salt.

Remove the pan from the heat and stir in the icing sugar
until the mixture is stiff and fudgy.

Line a small, shallow baking tin with baking parchment
and press the fudge into the tin. Smooth with the back
of a spoon and then refrigerate for at least 6 hours (or
overnight) until firm and set. Cut into bite-sized chunks
and dust with icing sugar.

TIPS

Vegan butter and peanut butter can have variations in
the amount of oil they contain, which may affect the
firmness of the fudge. If the mixture appears oily after
you have added the icing sugar, add a little more icing
sugar (up to 50g/2oz).

Cardamom-roasted persimmons with pistachios

SERVES 2 GENEROUSLY

3 tbsp **maple syrup**

pinch of ground **cardamom**

pinch of ground **cinnamon**

3 **persimmons**, quartered, tough tops removed

2 tbsp shelled **pistachios**, roughly chopped

I love the delicate, nutty flavour of persimmons, especially when they have been roasted with smoky maple syrup, cardamom and cinnamon. Top with pistachios, for added crunch.

Preheat the oven to 180°C/350°F/gas mark 4.

In a bowl, mix together the maple syrup, cardamom and cinnamon.

Dip the persimmon quarters into the spiced maple mix, then place into a deep roasting tin. Drizzle any remaining spiced maple syrup over the persimmon quarters. Cover loosely with foil, then roast in the oven for 30 minutes.

Remove from the oven and spoon into serving dishes. Scatter with the chopped pistachios.

TIPS
I like to serve these with a swirl of cool coconut yogurt.

Coconut panna cotta with mango coulis

SERVES 2

400ml (14fl oz) canned **coconut milk**

2 tbsp **caster (superfine) sugar**

1 tbsp **agar flakes**

3 tbsp **pineapple juice**

1 ripe **mango**, peeled, stoned and diced

Cool and creamy with a fruity topping, this panna cotta recipe has a tropical twist for a taste of the summer. Panna cotta is traditionally made with cream, which I've switched to coconut milk; and gelatine, for which I've substituted vegan-friendly agar. Agar is a thickener produced from seaweed, and will give your panna cotta the all-important set and 'wobble'!

Add the coconut milk, caster sugar and agar flakes to a pan and bring to a simmer over a low–medium heat for 4–5 minutes until you can see that all of the agar flakes have fully dissolved.

Pour the mixture into two 180ml (6fl oz) dariole moulds, then refrigerate overnight, or for at least 6 hours, to allow the mixture to set completely.

To make the mango coulis, add the pineapple juice and two-thirds of the diced mango to a pan and simmer for 10 minutes until softened and combined. Pour into a high-powered jug blender (or use a hand blender) and blitz until smooth. Chill for at least an hour.

Remove the panna cotta from the fridge and stand the moulds in a bowl of hot water for up to a minute, to make removal easier. Place the panna cotta moulds on serving plates and gently shake to allow the panna cotta to slide onto the plates.

Stir the remaining mango into the coulis, then pour over the panna cotta and serve immediately.

TIPS
Agar flakes are available in large supermarkets, and also in Chinese supermarkets.

Blood orange granita

SERVES 4

juice of 8 large unwaxed **blood oranges**

———————

juice of 2 unwaxed **lemons**

———————

50g (2oz) **caster (superfine) sugar**

———————

I love this refreshing, cooling granita, which is the perfect dessert or refreshing snack on a hot, summer's day. Unlike a smooth sorbet, the granita has broken ice crystals for revitalizing refreshment – and it's easier to prepare than you think.

Add the blood orange juice, lemon juice and sugar to a pan and simmer over a medium heat for 3–4 minutes until the sugar has dissolved.

Pour the mixture into a freezer-safe shallow dish and freeze for 1 hour.

After 1 hour, use a fork to break up the ice crystals, then return to the freezer for another 30 minutes. Again, run a fork through the ice to separate and break up the crystals, then return to the freezer for another 30 minutes.

After the final 30 minutes, fork through the granita one last time until all of the mixture is in icy crystals, then serve immediately.

TIPS
Bring the oranges and lemons to room temperature before using, to get maximum juice from the fruits.

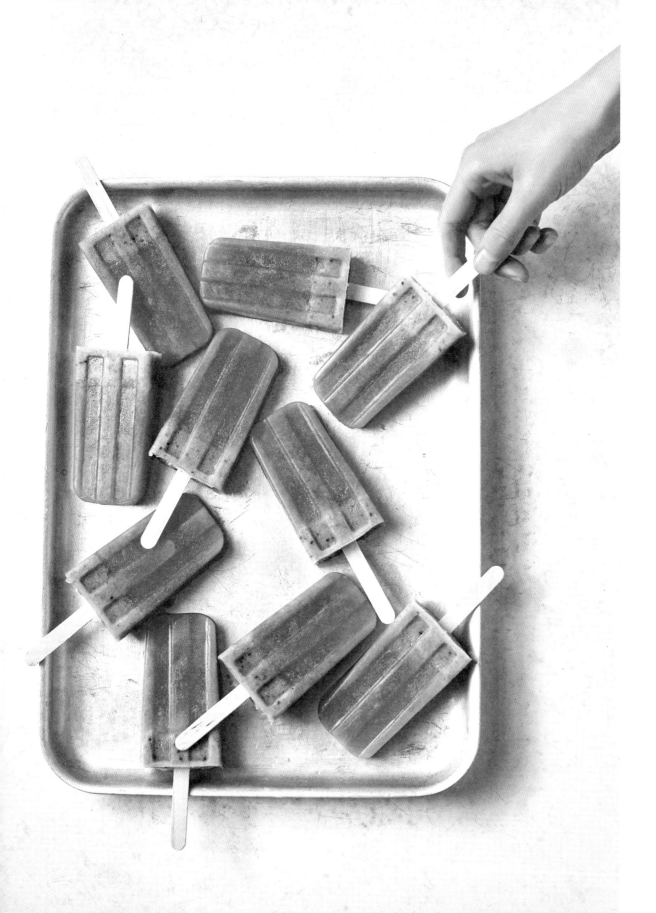

Watermelon ice lollies

MAKES ABOUT 8
LOLLIES

1 small **watermelon**, halved
and deseeded

———

2 **kiwi fruits**, peeled

———

1 tbsp **coconut yogurt**

———

small handful of **spinach**

———

These fruity, no-added-sugar lollies are the perfect sweet treat for grown-ups or little ones. Make them the day before and freeze overnight, for effortless summer refreshment.

Spoon the pink watermelon flesh into a high-powered jug blender (or spoon into a large bowl if you're using a hand blender) and blitz until smooth. Pour into ice-lolly moulds, leaving a 2cm (1in) gap at the top, then freeze for 4 hours.

Blitz the kiwis, coconut yogurt and spinach in the blender until smooth (or in a bowl with a hand blender).

Remove the lollies from the freezer and top each one up with the puréed kiwi mix. Freeze for another 4 hours, or overnight.

TIPS
Pour any remaining fruit purée into ice-cube trays, freeze, then add to a jug of water for a fruity refreshing drink.

Slow cooker spiced cider

SERVES 6

1.5 litres (2½ pints) good-quality
apple cider (ensure vegan)

4 **cinnamon** sticks

6 **star anise**

1 tbsp whole **cloves**

2 **red apples**,
halved and cored

Start enjoying this deliciously spiced cider in autumn, for a cosy, warming drink for every seasonal celebration. Use the 'keep warm' setting on your slow cooker to save you reheating for each guest.

Add all of the ingredients to a slow cooker. Cook on low for 4 hours until the cider is infused with spice.

Ladle into glasses or cups and enjoy warm.

TIPS

Always check that the cider is vegan friendly, as some varieties contain animal ingredients.

BASICS

Everyone needs a handful of essential vegan recipes including side dishes, dressings, sauces and dips. Make life simpler by using just five ingredients to create these easy yet delicious basics (I won't tell if you don't...).

Citrus tabbouleh

SERVES 4
as a side dish

80g (3oz) **bulgar wheat**

30g (1oz) **flat-leaf parsley**, finely chopped

1 unwaxed **orange**, peeled and chopped into 1cm (½in) pieces

juice of 1 unwaxed **lemon**

generous drizzle of good-quality extra virgin olive oil

generous pinch of sea salt

Everyone needs a great tabbouleh recipe; it's ideal as a salad, as part of a sharing platter or as a side to my harissa-yogurt whole roasted cauliflower with pomegranate and pistachios (page 97). This recipe has a fresh twist, with the addition of zesty orange, making it perfect for every season.

Scatter the bulgar wheat into a bowl and pour over enough boiling water to cover. Place a plate or some cling film over the top and allow to stand for 10–12 minutes until the water has been fully absorbed.

Fork through the bulgar wheat to separate the grains, then stir in the chopped parsley and orange pieces. Squeeze in the lemon juice and drizzle in the extra virgin olive oil, then stir to distribute evenly.

Season generously with sea salt and serve warm or cold.

TIPS
Ensure your citrus fruits are unwaxed, as the waxed varieties are not suitable for vegans.

Green apple salsa

MAKES 1 SMALL BOWL

2 **Granny Smith apples**, cored and finely chopped

1 small **red onion**, finely chopped

generous handful of **flat-leaf parsley**, finely chopped

juice of 1 unwaxed **lime**

½ small **red chilli**, deseeded and thinly sliced into rings

pinch of smoked sea salt

Give salsa a twist by adding crisp, green apples in place of the traditional tomato. Serve as a dip for tortilla chips, load into vegan cream cheese sandwiches or serve alongside chunky chilli (page 132).

In a large bowl, stir together the apples, red onion and parsley. Squeeze over the lime juice and stir through.

Scatter over the red chilli, then season with smoked sea salt to taste.

TIPS

There's no need to peel the apples; the vibrant green colour is so appetizing, and what's more, the skin is a great source of fibre!

Classic coleslaw

SERVES 4
as a side dish

½ **white cabbage**, finely
shredded

———

1 small **red onion**, thinly sliced

———

2 **carrots**, peeled and shredded

———

juice of ½ unwaxed **lemon**

———

3 tbsp vegan **mayonnaise**

———

Forget fancy slaws, sometimes all you need is a classic coleslaw – crunchy, creamy and zesty. Load into slow cooker jacket potatoes (page 202) or serve with vegan burgers at a barbecue. This coleslaw will stay fresh in the fridge for up to 2 days.

In a bowl, mix together the cabbage, onion and carrots. Squeeze over the lemon juice and leave to infuse for 10 minutes.

Stir through the vegan mayonnaise until all of the vegetables are generously coated.

TIPS
You'll find egg-free, vegan-friendly mayonnaise in most supermarkets, including varieties from well-known brands.

Baba ganoush

MAKES 1 BOWL

2 large **aubergines (eggplants)**, skins pricked with a fork and halved

2 tbsp sunflower oil

1 tbsp good-quality **tahini**

2 **garlic** cloves, crushed

pinch of smoked sea salt and black pepper

zest and juice of 1 unwaxed **lemon**

small handful of **flat-leaf parsley**, finely chopped

This perfectly smoky and satisfying dip is best served with my easy flatbreads (page 194) or toasted pitta breads and vegetable crudités. Delicious as a side dish to parsnip and chickpea tagine (page 130).

Preheat the oven to 180°C/350°F/gas mark 4.

Place the aubergine halves on a baking tray and drizzle with the oil. Bake in the oven for 45–50 minutes until softened. Carefully remove the aubergines from the oven and allow to cool fully.

Once the aubergines have cooled, use a spoon to scoop out the softened flesh into a bowl. Stir in the tahini to combine, then mix in the garlic, smoked sea salt and black pepper and lemon juice. Spoon into a serving bowl and scatter with the flat-leaf parsley and lemon zest.

TIPS

In summer months, barbecue the aubergines whole for 15–20 minutes for a smokier flavour; allow to cool before halving and scooping out the flesh.

Cheat's ultimate houmous

SERVES 4

2 tbsp shelled **pistachios**, roughly chopped

2 x 200g (7oz) tubs of good-quality **houmous**

generous glug of good-quality extra virgin olive oil

seeds from 1 ripe **pomegranate**

handful of **flat-leaf parsley**, roughly chopped

It's great to make houmous from scratch, when you have the time and inclination to soak and boil chickpeas, and then blitz with tahini, garlic, lemon juice and extra virgin olive oil. But when you don't, make the ultimate dip by enhancing your favourite shop-bought houmous. (I won't tell if you don't!) Serve with toasted pitta breads and crudités for lunch.

Toast the pistachios in a dry pan for 2–3 minutes until you notice a nutty aroma. Remove them from the pan before they start to burn.

Spoon the houmous into a serving bowl and stir through the extra virgin olive oil.

Scatter over the pomegranate seeds and flat-leaf parsley, then top with the toasted pistachios.

5-minute fried rice

SERVES 2
as a side dish

1 tbsp sunflower oil

---

5 **button mushrooms**,
brushed clean and halved

---

2 tbsp frozen or fresh
edamame beans

6–8 tbsp leftover cooked
basmati rice (or pre-cooked
basmati rice)

---

1 tbsp dark **soy sauce**

---

zest and juice of
½ unwaxed **lime**

If you're looking for a way to use up that leftover rice, then look no further than this simple and tasty fried rice. Serve as a side to sticky marmalade tofu (page 94) for an Eastern feast, or enjoy in a bowl for a quick lunch.

Heat the oil in a wok over a high heat, then throw in the mushrooms. Stir-fry for 1 minute, then add the edamame beans and stir-fry for a further minute.

Add the basmati rice and soy sauce and cook for another 2 minutes, stirring frequently.

Remove from the heat, then sprinkle in the lime zest and juice. Serve hot.

Pictured on page 94

TIPS
For extra freshness, throw in a small handful of coriander (cilantro) leaves before serving.

Pilau rice

SERVES 4
as a side dish

300g (10oz) **basmati rice**

500ml (18fl oz) hot
vegetable stock (page 212)

½ tsp ground **turmeric**

1 **cinnamon** stick

2 **bay** leaves

Delicately flavoured, vibrantly coloured and so simple to prepare, pilau rice is the perfect accompaniment to speedy chickpea masala (page 101).

Add all of the ingredients to a large pan and bring to a simmer over a medium heat. Cook for 15 minutes, stirring occasionally to avoid sticking.

When all of the stock has been absorbed, remove the pan from the heat, then cover the pan with a lid. Leave to stand for 5 minutes.

Remove and discard the cinnamon stick and bay leaves. Fork through the rice to separate the grains and serve hot.

Pictured on page 102

TIPS

Once cooked, allow the rice to stand for 5 minutes, covered with the pan lid, to absorb any remaining stock and flavours from the spices.

Easy flatbreads

MAKES 8

250g (9oz) **self-raising flour**, plus extra for dusting

250g (9oz) **unsweetened soya yogurt**

1 tbsp sunflower oil

These rustic flatbreads are so easy to make, you'll never need to buy them again! The trick is to get the pan really hot before you cook each flatbread, then keep an eye out for the classic golden-brown patches to appear. Serve with parsnip and chickpea tagine (page 130).

In a large bowl, mix together the flour and soya yogurt to form a dough, bringing it together with your hands towards the end. Set aside to rest for 30 minutes at room temperature.

Lightly dust a clean work surface with flour and cut the dough in half. Cut each half into four pieces. Use a rolling pin to roll each piece to the size of a small plate.

Heat a flat pan over a medium-high heat until hot. Rub each doughy flatbread with a little oil, then use tongs to place onto the hot pan. Cook for 20–30 seconds until golden-brown patches appear. Carefully turn the flatbread and cook the other side for 20–30 seconds. Repeat until each flatbread is cooked. Serve warm or at room temperature.

3-ingredient beer bread

MAKES 1 SMALL LOAF

450g (1lb) **self-raising flour**

1 tbsp **granulated sugar**

330ml (11fl oz) bottle
of **beer** (ensure vegan)

Lazy bakers rejoice! This 3-ingredient bread recipe takes under an hour to become a delicious loaf – and it requires no kneading or proving. The magic/science lies in the beer: the yeast reacts with the sugar and the fizzy bubbles add extra carbon dioxide, meaning you'll get a fluffy, tearable loaf, with a satisfying crust.

Preheat the oven to 180°C/350°F/gas mark 4. Line a small 23 x 12cm (9 x 5in) loaf tin with baking parchment.

Mix together the flour and sugar in a large bowl. Pour in the beer and mix to form a thick batter. Stir to ensure the mixture is combined, then pour into the lined loaf tin.

Bake in the oven for 50–55 minutes until a golden crust has formed. Allow to cool a little before removing from the tin and peeling away the baking parchment.

Pictured on page 32

TIPS

The type of beer used affects the flavour of the loaf. Dark ales create a complex and deep flavour. I love using a good-quality IPA, which gives an almost bitter, sourdough taste. Or give beer the boot and add cider to the mix for a sweet loaf. Whatever you choose, ensure it is vegan, as some beers and ciders use animal ingredients in the brewing process.

Yorkshire puddings

MAKES ABOUT 8

Suitable for freezing

200g (7oz) **plain (all-purpose) flour**, sifted

½ tsp **baking powder**

---

pinch of fine sea salt

400ml (14fl oz) **unsweetened soya milk**, chilled

---

8 tsp sunflower oil

What's a Sunday roast without a Yorkshire pudding? Serve alongside roasted carrots with maple and pecans (page 198) and gratin dauphinoise (page 200) as substantial sides to your vegan roast, or serve midweek with your favourite vegan sausages and mushroom gravy (page 211).

In a large jug, stir together the flour, baking powder and sea salt. Pour in the soya milk and use a hand whisk to mix until smooth. Chill the batter in the fridge for 1 hour.

Preheat the oven to 220°C/425°F/gas mark 7.

Spoon 1 teaspoon of oil into each hole of an eight-hole muffin tin and place in the oven for 5–7 minutes until the oil is very hot.

Carefully remove the hot muffin tin from the oven and pour in the batter, to half-fill each hole. Return to the oven and cook for 30 minutes until golden and risen.

After 30 minutes, turn off the oven but leave the Yorkshire puddings inside to stand for a further 5 minutes. Then open the oven door slightly and allow to stand for another 5 minutes (this will ensure the Yorkshire puddings stay risen until they reach your plate). Serve hot.

TIPS
Using an eight-hole muffin tin makes small, individual Yorkshire puddings. If you want them to be larger, use a four-hole Yorkshire pudding tin, found in cookware shops.

Perfect roast potatoes

SERVES 4

8 tbsp sunflower oil

_____

4 large **baking potatoes**, peeled and quartered

_____

1 tbsp **plain (all-purpose) flour**

_____

generous pinch of sea salt

_____

The perfect roast potato may seem like a tricky task to master, but it is in fact very simple. Crisp and golden on the outside, fluffy on the inside and with a taste of home. Serve straight from the oven with your Sunday lunch, or as a comforting side to my sausage, sage and bean casserole (page 106).

Preheat the oven to 200°C/400°F/gas mark 6.

Drizzle the oil into a deep roasting tin, then place in the oven for 10 minutes to heat up while you prepare the potatoes for roasting.

Add the potato quarters to a large pan and pour over enough boiling water to cover them. Parboil the potatoes for 5 minutes, then drain them thoroughly and return them to the pan.

Sprinkle the flour over the potatoes, then cover the pan with a lid. Shake the pan vigorously to coat all the surfaces of the potatoes.

Carefully remove the roasting tin of hot oil from the oven. Use tongs to place each potato into the oil, turning to ensure each surface is coated.

Roast in the oven for 40 minutes, then increase the heat to 220°C/425°F/gas mark 7 for a further 10 minutes. Season with sea salt just before serving.

TIPS
Fluffy potatoes such as King Edward and Maris Piper make the best roast potatoes, every time.

Roasted carrots with maple and pecans

SERVES 4
as a side dish

8 **carrots**, scrubbed

2 tbsp sunflower oil

4 tbsp **maple syrup**

6 **pecans**, roughly chopped

small handful of
coriander (cilantro)

pinch of sea salt
and black pepper

Show the humble carrot some love with caramelized maple syrup and oven-toasted pecans. Roasted vegetables will never be the same again! Serve on a Sunday with Yorkshire puddings (page 196) or any day with leek and mushroom pot pies (page 120).

Preheat the oven to 200°C/400°F/gas mark 6.

Place the whole carrots in a roasting tin and drizzle over the oil. Roast in the oven for 20 minutes.

Carefully remove the tin from the oven and drizzle with the maple syrup. Scatter with the chopped pecans and cover the tin loosely with foil. Return the tin to the oven for a further 20–25 minutes until the carrots have softened.

Scatter with the coriander and season with sea salt and black pepper. Serve hot.

TIPS
Parsnips make an excellent alternative to carrots in this recipe (especially for Christmas dinner).

Gratin dauphinoise

as a side dish

3 **baking potatoes**, peeled
and very thinly sliced

———

200ml (7fl oz) **soya
single cream**

———

200ml (7fl oz) **unsweetened
soya milk**

———

½ tsp **thyme** leaves,
finely chopped

———

1 **garlic** clove, crushed

———

generous pinch of sea salt
and black pepper

———

**These luxurious layered potatoes are the perfect side
dish for your Sunday dinner. You'll find soya cream in
most supermarkets, making it easy to create decadent
dishes like this.**

Preheat the oven to 200°C/400°F/gas mark 6.

Blot the potato slices with paper towels or a clean dish
towel to remove excess moisture. Arrange the slices in
three layers in a flat baking dish.

In a pan, whisk together the soya cream, soya milk, thyme
leaves and garlic. Gently heat over a low heat until
combined – do not let it come to the boil. Pour the creamy
sauce generously over the layered potatoes and cover
loosely with foil. Bake in the oven for 1½ hours.

Carefully remove from the oven and season with sea salt
and black pepper before serving.

TIPS

It's worth using fresh thyme in this recipe, for a bigger
fragrance and flavour. Simply drag your thumb and finger
down the length of the thyme sprig to easily remove
the leaves.

Colcannon mash

SERVES 4

4 **baking potatoes**, peeled
and roughly chopped

½ medium **Savoy cabbage**,
finely shredded

3 tbsp vegan **butter**

4 tbsp **soya single cream**

3 **spring onions (scallions)**,
thinly sliced

pinch of sea salt
and black pepper

If you thought Irish colcannon mash couldn't possibly
be vegan, then think again. This comforting and creamy
side dish takes mashed potatoes to a new level, with the
addition of leafy greens and pops of spring onion. King
Edward or Maris Piper potatoes are the best potatoes
to use for velvety mash. You'll find soya single cream
readily available in supermarkets, often both fresh and
UHT. Serve with vegan sausages and mushroom gravy
(page 211) for a simple supper.

Bring a large lidded pan of water to the boil, then add
the potatoes. Boil for 10 minutes with the lid loosely
placed over.

Add the shredded cabbage to the pan and cook for a
further 10 minutes until the potatoes have softened.
Remove from the heat and thoroughly drain away the
water. Return both the potatoes and cabbage to the pan.

Add the vegan butter and soya cream, then mash the
potatoes and cabbage until semi-smooth, or with no large
lumps of potato remaining.

Stir through the spring onions and season with sea salt
and black pepper to taste.

Pictured on page 106

TIP No Savoy cabbage? Kale or cavolo nero make excellent
substitutes here.

Slow cooker jacket potatoes

4 large **baking potatoes**,
scrubbed clean and dried
thoroughly

———

1 tbsp olive oil

———

pinch of sea salt
and black pepper

———

**Pop these potatoes into the slow cooker first thing in
the morning and have delicious jacket potatoes in time
for lunch. These baked potatoes are perfectly crisp on
the outside, and fluffy on the inside.**

Pierce the potatoes with a fork a few times, then rub over
the olive oil. Season with sea salt and black pepper.

Wrap each potato in a piece of foil, then place in the slow
cooker. Cover with the lid and bake on high for 5 hours
until cooked through.

TIPS

For an alternative filling to simple vegan butter, fill with
coronation chickpeas (page 57).

Black pepper croutons

SERVES 2 GENEROUSLY

2 thick slices of **bread** (about
1 day old), crusts trimmed, cut
into even cubes

———

2 tbsp good-quality olive oil

———

pinch of black pepper

———

**Add crunch to soups and salads with croutons, which are
so easy to make – you'll never have to buy them again.
It's worth using a good-quality olive oil for this recipe,
as the croutons take on some of the flavours. Delicious
with tomato and chilli soup (page 34).**

Preheat the oven to 180°C/350°F/gas mark 4.

Toss the bread, olive oil and black pepper together in
a bowl, then tip onto a baking tray in a single layer.

Bake in the oven for 8–10 minutes until the croutons are
golden and crunchy.

Pictured on page 34

TIPS
These croutons will keep fresh for up to 3 days in a
sealed container.

Maple and mustard jar dressing

2 tbsp **maple syrup**

1 tbsp **wholegrain mustard**

1 tbsp **cider vinegar**

8 tbsp sunflower oil

generous pinch of sea salt

It's good to have a basic dressing to hand, for when you want to liven up a salad, or add flavour to boiled new potatoes. This dressing balances sweet and sharp with a hint of acidity, making this dressing your new go-to.

Add all of the ingredients to a clean jar with a tight-fitting lid. Screw on the lid tightly and shake very vigorously for 1 minute until combined.

TIPS
Sunflower oil is used here, as its neutral flavour lets the maple and mustard shine through, but you could replace it with olive oil if you prefer.

Versatile tomato sauce

MAKES ABOUT 900ML
(1½ PINTS)

Suitable for freezing

1 tbsp olive oil

3 **garlic** cloves, crushed

800g (1lb 12oz) good-quality canned **chopped tomatoes**

2 tbsp **tomato purée (paste)**

1 tsp granulated **sugar**

60g (2¼oz) **basil**, leaves and stalks finely chopped

generous pinch of sea salt and black pepper

I always have this speedy sauce available in the freezer or fridge. It is delicious on pasta, or as a base for pantry minestrone (page 22). This recipe fills approximately three containers with 300ml (10fl oz) sauce (the perfect quantity for each recipe). It refrigerates well for up to 5 days, and freezes for up to 3 months. Feel free to blend the sauce to make it silky smooth, or keep it chunkier for a more rustic version.

Heat the oil and garlic in a large pan over a low–medium heat for 2 minutes until the garlic has softened and infused the oil.

Pour in the chopped tomatoes and add 250ml (9fl oz) cold water. Stir through the tomato purée and sugar, then add a lid to the pan and simmer for 20 minutes.

Remove the lid from the pan and stir in the chopped basil. Simmer for a further 5 minutes.

Remove from the heat and season with sea salt and black pepper to taste. Allow to cool fully, then blitz in a high-powdered jug blender (or use a hand blender) until smooth, if desired, before pouring into clean jars for refrigerating or plastic containers for freezing.

TIPS

No tomato purée? Tomato ketchup will add concentrated flavour and instant seasoning.

Simple korma sauce

SERVES 4

Suitable for freezing

1 tbsp sunflower oil

_____

1 **onion**, finely diced

_____

2 **garlic** cloves, crushed

_____

2 tbsp mild **curry paste**
(ensure dairy free)

_____

800ml (28fl oz) canned
coconut milk

_____

2 tbsp **flaked almonds**

_____

pinch of sea salt

_____

Use this mild and creamy sauce to whip up any korma in under half an hour! Throw in chickpeas or cauliflower or create my favourite Boxing Day korma with leftover roasted vegetables. Finish with a squeeze of lime juice and top with coriander (cilantro) for an added layer of freshness. Serve with vegan naan breads.

Heat the oil in a large pan, add the onion and cook over a medium heat for 2–3 minutes until it begins to soften. Add the garlic and cook for a further minute.

Stir through the curry paste to coat the onion and garlic. Pour in the coconut milk and stir, then reduce the heat slightly and allow to simmer for 15 minutes until thickened.

In the meantime, toast the flaked almonds in a dry pan until golden and fragrant.

Remove the sauce from the heat and stir through the toasted almonds, then season to taste with sea salt.

TIPS

Flaked almonds give the best crunch and toasted flavour, although peanuts and cashews also work well in this sauce. It's worth the effort to toast the almonds in a separate pan, for a deep flavour and lightly crisp texture.

Satay sauce

SERVES 2

Suitable for freezing

4 tbsp smooth **peanut butter**

———

½ tsp dried **chilli flakes**

———

1 tbsp dark **soy sauce**

———

2 **spring onions (scallions)**,
finely chopped

———

juice of 1 unwaxed **lime**

———

**Don't spend money on pricey pre-made satay sauce
when you already have the ingredients in your store
cupboard. Keep a tub of this in the fridge or freezer to
add to a stir-fry, use as a dipping sauce for aubergine
tempura (page 61) or drizzle over vegetable kebabs.**

Add the peanut butter, chilli flakes and soy sauce to a pan,
then pour in 200ml (7fl oz) just-boiled water. Simmer over
a low–medium heat for 8–10 minutes, mixing with a small
balloon whisk to combine.

Remove from the heat and stir in the spring onions and
lime juice.

Pictured on page 60

TIPS The sauce may separate slightly during the freezing
process, but will combine again once heated.

Béchamel sauce

SERVES 4
(or enough for one lasagne)

2 tbsp sunflower oil

2 tbsp **plain (all-purpose) flour**

500ml (18fl oz) **unsweetened soya milk**, warmed

pinch of freshly grated **nutmeg**

pinch of sea salt

Every cook needs to know how to make the perfect béchamel sauce – and it's not as tricky as you'd think. While the ingredients are switched up to be vegan friendly, the preparation principles remain the same. Whip up a vegan lasagne by layering egg-free pasta sheets with simple Bolognese (page 117) and lashings of this sauce before baking for 35–40 minutes at 200°C/400°F/gas mark 6.

Heat the oil in a pan over a low-medium heat, then add the flour. Use a balloon whisk to mix into a roux (when the oil and flour have combined into a paste).

Pour 100ml (3½fl oz) of the warmed soya milk into the pan and whisk continuously for 2–3 minutes until the mixture begins to thicken. Repeat this step by pouring in 100ml (3½fl oz) each time and whisking continuously until all of the milk has been used.

Once the sauce has thickened and is smooth, stir in the nutmeg and sea salt to taste.

TIPS

Warming the soya milk reduces the risk of any lumps in the sauce; I do this by heating it for 20 seconds in a microwave. Don't panic if you do end up with any lumps – simply strain the sauce before using.

Mushroom gravy

SERVES 4

Suitable for freezing

1 tbsp sunflower oil

_____

250g (9oz) **chestnut (cremini) mushrooms**, brushed clean and thinly sliced

_____

1 small **onion**, finely diced

_____

100ml (3½fl oz) **red wine** (ensure vegan)

_____

2 tbsp **plain (all-purpose) flour**

_____

500ml (18fl oz) hot **vegetable stock** (page 212)

_____

generous pinch of black pepper

_____

Who knew homemade gravy could be so simple to make? I love this rich gravy to have slices of mushroom visible when pouring, but if you prefer it to be completely smooth, simply strain before serving. Be patient and allow the mushrooms to brown in the pan, to really bring out their depth of flavour. Serve generously over my pear and butter bean traybake (page 118).

Heat the oil in a pan, add the mushrooms and cook over a medium heat for 5 minutes, stirring frequently, until softened and browned. Add the onion and cook for a further 2–3 minutes until softened.

Add the red wine and flour and cook, stirring continuously, for 1 minute.

Pour in the vegetable stock and simmer for 15 minutes. Use a balloon whisk to stir and mix frequently to avoid the gravy sticking.

When thickened, remove from the heat and season to taste with black pepper. Allow to stand for 10 minutes to let it further thicken before serving.

TIPS

Don't be tempted to add more flour at any point; the gravy will thicken as it cooks and also continue to thicken as it cools.

Homemade vegetable stock

MAKES ABOUT 1.5
LITRES (2½ PINTS)

Suitable for freezing

4 **celery** sticks, roughly chopped

4 **carrots**, washed and roughly chopped

2 **onions**, halved

1 tbsp dried **herbes de Provence**

2 tsp black **peppercorns**

generous pinch of sea salt

Vegetable stock is readily available from supermarkets, although it can sometimes contain cow's milk products, artificial flavour enhancers and excess salt. Making your own vegetable stock is so easy, very cheap and means that you always have control of exactly what is in it! I freeze stock in 500ml (18fl oz) quantities, perfect to add to soups and casseroles.

Add all of the ingredients to a large pan and cover with 2 litres (3½ pints) cold water. Bring to the boil, then simmer over a low heat for 2 hours.

Remove from the heat and strain the stock into jugs or another large bowl, discarding the softened vegetables. If the stock is to be frozen, ladle or pour into clean containers and allow to cool fully before freezing.

TIPS
Add in any extra vegetable peelings you have available, for additional flavour. I freeze all vegetable peelings (except potato) and simply add them into the pan. There's plenty of flavour in those skins that would otherwise end up in the bin!

Quick-pickled onions

SERVES 4

2 **red onions**, thinly sliced
into rings

200ml (7fl oz) **cider vinegar**

1 tbsp **maple syrup**

½ tsp dried **chilli flakes**

zest of 1 unwaxed **lime**

generous pinch of sea salt

**Sometimes a dish calls for zingy, feisty pickled onions.
Try them on top of creamy coconut dhal (page 100),
loaded over coronation chickpeas (page 57) or to add
tanginess to baked sweet potato enchiladas (page 134).**

Put the onion rings into a large bowl and pour over
enough boiling water to cover completely (this takes away
the initial sharpness of the onions). Leave to stand for 10
minutes while you prepare the vinegar.

In a jug, whisk together the vinegar and maple syrup, then
stir in the chilli flakes, lime zest and sea salt.

Drain the water from the onions and pat dry with paper
towels. Pour over the vinegar mixture, then refrigerate for
1 hour before serving.

Pictured on page 136

TIPS
Quick-pickled onions are best enjoyed within 2 weeks.
Simply pour into a clean jar and keep refrigerated.

Index

Katy Beskow

Katy Beskow is an award-winning cook, writer and cookery tutor with a passion for seasonal ingredients, vibrant food and fuss-free home cooking. Once inspired by a bustling and colourful fruit market in South London, Katy now lives in rural Yorkshire and cooks from a small (yet perfectly functioning) kitchen. She blogs at www.katybeskow.com. Katy is the author of *15 Minute Vegan* (2017), *15 Minute Vegan Comfort Food* (2018) and *15 Minute Vegan on a Budget* (2019); this is her fourth book.

Acknowledgements

Firstly, a heartfelt thank you to all of the incredible team at Quadrille Publishing. Thank you to publishing director Sarah Lavelle for commissioning this book, and for believing in me. I feel so lucky that this is my job, and it wouldn't be possible without you. Words cannot describe how grateful and thankful I am to editor Harriet Webster. Your attention to detail, logical approach and top-notch communication has made working on this book an absolute pleasure. Thank you for your guidance at each stage, and for always going the extra mile. I can't wait to work with you again! Further thanks to Clare Sayer for editorial support.

Huge thank you to talented designer Emily Lapworth and all of the design team at Quadrille Publishing for the modern vision and layout of the book. It is just beautiful, and everything I hoped the book would be.

I am so grateful for the hard work of publicists Rebecca Smedley and Emma Marijewycz. Thank you for being wonderful to work with, for championing the books and for your support at events. Special thanks to Laura Willis and Laura Eldridge for your ongoing expertise and guidance. Thank you to Fran White and Hazel Henbury of Luna PR for keeping me busy between books with social media and wonderful projects.

Thank you to photographer Luke Albert for the incredible images throughout this book, and for your patience to get the perfect cover shot. It was a pleasure to work with

you! Huge thank you to food stylist Tamara Vos for bringing the recipes to life in such a beautiful way, and for bringing so much fun (and epic playlists) to the shoot. Thank you also to assistant food stylists Sophie Pryn and Sophie Garwood for your hard work and attention to detail throughout. Thank you to Danni Hooker for the fabulous hair and make-up, and for putting me at ease with lots of chat and laughs! I will always remember those surprisingly sunny spring days, eating lunch together, alfresco, in SE17.

Ongoing thanks to my wonderful literary agent Victoria Hobbs at A. M. Heath. Without your belief in me, none of this would be possible! Thank you for your expert advice, guidance and on-point Netflix recommendations.

To my lovely best friends Mary-Anne, Charlotte, Louise, Amelia, Emma, Amy and Katie – thank you for the chats, coffees and encouragement to pursue my dreams. Thank you to Dudley, the house rabbit, for being the best writing partner anyone could ask for. Thank you to David for full use of the kitchen, tidying up properly and reminding me to use the extractor fan.

Loving thanks to my fabulous mum and dad, who support me with love and encouragement through every step of this journey. Thank you to my beautiful sister Carolyne, and brilliant brother-in-law Mark for believing in me (and trying all of the recipes!). To my incredible nieces Tamzin

and Tara – my hungriest house guests and biggest critics. You're growing into such caring, nurturing girls, and I love you very much. Thank you for always being excited when you find my books in the library. Thank you to Auntie May for your love and support. I couldn't do this without my wonderful family!

Finally, heartfelt thank you to everyone who has bought this book. I hope it inspires you to make simple, delicious dishes that will become regular staples in your kitchen for many years to come.

Publishing Director
Sarah Lavelle

Editor
Harriet Webster

Copy Editor
Clare Sayer

Art Direction and Design
Emily Lapworth

Design Assistant
Christine Geiger

Photographer
Luke Albert

Food Stylist
Tamara Vos

Prop Stylist
Linda Berlin

Make-up Artist
Dani Hooker

Production Director
Vincent Smith

Production Controller
Sinead Hering

First published in 2019 by Quadrille,
an imprint of Hardie Grant Publishing

Quadrille
52–54 Southwark Street
London SE1 1UN
quadrille.com

The rights of Katy Beskow to be identified as the
author of this work have been asserted by her
in accordance with the Copyright, Design and
Patents Act 1988.

Cataloguing in Publication Data: a catalogue
record for this book is available from the British
Library.

UK ISBN: 978 1 78713 431 7
US + Export ISBN: 978 1 78713 528 4

Reprinted in 2019 (twice)
10 9 8 7 6 5 4 3

Printed in Italy by Elcograf S.P.A